Never Apologize for Your Tears

One Woman's Mission to Make Grief Normal

Lisa Orris

Dedication

To my first-born son, Billy. You changed me as a woman and mother, in life and in death. I love you always.

Table of Contents

Foreword

In my more than 30 years as a Licensed Professional Christian Counselor, I have worked with countless men and women through intense seasons of grief and loss.

Over the last six months, I have had the privilege of walking alongside two close friends whose spouses died. Both of them experienced a roller coaster of raw emotions—sadness, fear, confusion, aloneness—and just want their pain to go away and be in the past. They are trying to pick up the pieces of their lives and put them back together. My dear friends would have benefited greatly from reading *Never Apologize For Your Tears*.

I am so thankful to God for leading Lisa to write this amazing book. It is one of the best books on grief that I have ever read and will touch so many lives while normalizing the experiences of grief.

I have known the Orris family for more than 25 years. As I was beginning my career as a Professional Christian Counselor in the mid 1990s, I was seeking churches with which to associate and offer my services. This search eventually led me to Lisa and Bill, and I have maintained a professional relationship with them through these years. I became somewhat of a spiritual mentor to Lisa as she and Bill pursued their ministry callings through serving local churches.

They have pastored several churches which partnered with White Stone Resources Ltd., the Christian Counseling practice that I founded and owned for 25 years. We have shared many hours of learning together how to help those in the church deal with the hurts and struggles of their lives. I am so honored to be asked by Lisa to write this foreword to her first book, as I have so much respect for her, and for Bill, as they have navigated the very deep and tumultuous waters of grief in the aftermath of the tragic death of their son, Billy, and later the sudden death of their daughter-in-law, Kierra.

Throughout the book, Lisa's writing gives the reader permission to just be … To be broken, to be sad, to be a mess for as long as is needed. In my many years as a Counselor, I have come to believe that God created each of us as a human being. His greatest desire is that we be who and what He made us to be: His. In the midst of whatever life brings to us, no matter how difficult, we belong to Him.

We are all born into a world that teaches us to become human "doings" and to apply various formulas to every set of struggles we encounter for the purpose of solving or bringing them to resolution. But Lisa opposes that, telling readers to let themselves experience and embrace their process of grief. She gives the reader permission to be raw and real! Lisa challenges many of the historical myths of the grief process and offers practical "Grief Practices" for the reader to use on his or her journey. Robert Frost writes in his poem Servant to Servants, "The best way out is always through." Lisa helps each reader grow in their learning of how to go through their grief rather than working to get past it or out of it.

The great theologian, Oswald Chambers writes that "when there are trials in our lives, God is not trying to teach us something, but there is something He wants us to unlearn." This implies that the majority of trials in our lives are due to faulty learning. Through Lisa's writing, she helps the reader identify what needs to be "unlearned" for them to have a healthy processing of the loss they have experienced. These themes of being and unlearning are the core messages of Lisa's writing. Be where you are emotionally, and know that you are loved perfectly and completely by your Creator, Lord, and Savior.

My hope and prayer for you as a reader is that your life will be set more free to go through your grief and know that it is precious to God. The Psalmist writes in Psalm 56:8, "You have kept count of my tossings; put my tears in your bottle. Are they not in your book?" Yes, the Creator of all keeps our tears in His bottle and records them in His book.

I encourage you to embrace this book and be comforted by the freedom to be … and once you have read it, recommend it or pass it on to anyone you know that can benefit from the wisdom offered through these stories of Lisa and Bill's lives.

Raymond C. Wunderlich, M.Div., M.A.
Licensed Clinical Professional Counselor
Owner – Wunderlich Counseling & Consulting Ltd.

Chapter 1

Third Garage

I will never forget the way my husband paced back and forth in the ER next to our son lying lifeless on a gurney. He kept praying over and over again, begging God to raise our child from the dead. He was bawling uncontrollably and trying everything he knew to make it not be real. We were there for what seemed like hours and hours until we finally had to leave. During our drive home we sat in deafening silence. It was dark and eerie outside and we were completely without hope.

Billy changed my life. I wasn't at all sure about motherhood. My career had direction, my goals were clear, and motherhood felt like a foreign land. Still, after nearly three years of marriage, it seemed time to start a family. I mean that's what everyone does, right? One afternoon, nine months pregnant, I sat at the top of our staircase. I had just finished folding tiny onesies and stacking impossibly small socks into drawers. The sight of them undid me. I sank onto the step and began to sob. Picking up the phone, I called Bill, and through tears confessed, "I don't think I can go through with this." It was a little late for second thoughts.

When Billy was born—our firstborn, our everything—I was overcome not only with love, but also inadequacy. That first year I felt like I was fumbling over myself at every turn. Every decision felt heavy, every moment uncertain, and I had no idea how much babies cry for no reason! I adored him, but I had no roadmap, no confidence, no idea what I was doing. But that's when I began to change. I was forced to embrace who I really was.

Not a woman with an education, a title, or a position, but someone who was deeply loved by God and now called to be a mom … Billy's mom. I felt so alone and isolated in those early months that I talked to Billy incessantly. I am pretty sure this is why he talked at the young age of 10 months and probably why he grew up to be the articulate, expressive young man he was. It seemed from that moment on he never stopped talking. In fact, his verbal skills got him into trouble a lot! I remember that I could tell what kind of day we would have just by the way he would eat his cereal in the morning. Often I would look at him and tell him, "I will win today!" His curiosity and investigative mind only continued to show itself when he came home from kindergarten one day and looked at me and said, "Do reindeers really fly?"

I loved so many things about Billy. He was this beautiful mixture of fierce determination and tenderhearted compassion. Headstrong and focused, he threw himself at life like a bull charging forward—so much so that I often called him "Billy the Bull." He went at everything five hundred miles an hour, sometimes tripping over his own feet, blurting out words before thinking them through, making mistakes— but always quick to recognize when he'd hurt someone he loved. And when he did, his humility and compassion shone through.

Over the years, we had countless conversations about his attitude and how it seemed to land him in trouble. Not long ago, I came across one of his old journal entries from eighth grade. We read it together on his last birthday. In it, he wrote, My mom says if I keep up this attitude it will get me nowhere in life. We laughed so hard—it was so perfectly, unmistakably Billy. Yet even as we laughed, I could see the ways he was becoming the young man I had always prayed for: deeply devoted to his family, rooted in his faith, and living into the meaning of his name—William, the protector. That's exactly who he was to all of us.

Billy's faith ran deep and complicated. He passionately studied Scripture and constantly challenged us to look beyond what we had always been told. He refused to accept the status quo of Christianity or the Church. If anyone could defend their faith, it was Billy. Some of my most intense debates—about faith, about Scripture, about the Church—were with him. He pursued truth with relentless determination, sometimes driving me crazy with his convictions, but always pushing me not to settle. He wanted me to seek and discover for myself the deeper things of God.

Billy's passion for life was unrelenting—sometimes overwhelming, yet profoundly admirable. He was fearless in ways that amazed me, stretched me, and, at times, even scared me. He lived with a restless urgency, always reaching for more, always searching for truth, always pulling the rest of us along with him. As the oldest, he proudly carried the title of "third parent." He was the one who gathered us together and chose to live close by. He wanted us woven into the fabric of his daily life. Billy's presence anchored our family in ways I didn't fully realize until it was gone. When he died, it wasn't just his life we lost—it was also the countless ways he held us together, the unique place he filled in our family story. They say there's always an empty chair at the table. Always a hole in your heart when someone you love is gone. But the truth is, I don't have words for the loss of my firstborn son. No analogy or language could ever capture the constant ache I carry living each day without him.

Bill and I were told that couples tend to either move toward or away from each other in grief. That warning stayed with us. According to a study by The Compassionate Friends, 72% of bereaved parents said their marriage became more emotionally strained, and 16% reported separation or divorce after loss. Not wanting to become part of that statistic, we reached out to a counselor we had seen off and on through the years—a wise, steady presence in our lives.

He encouraged us to honor each other's grief and to remember that no two people will experience loss the same way, even as a married couple who shared a child.

My husband and I are wired differently. Always have been. But we're also a lot alike: both firstborns, both strong-willed, both used to being right. Our marriage has had no shortage of intense conversations over the years (and that's the polite way of putting it). We've fought hard for our connection. And in this season, we had to fight even harder. Sometimes that looked like giving space. Sometimes it looked like coming back together when neither of us knew what to say.

I learned quickly what our counselor meant. What brought Bill comfort didn't comfort me at all and the same was true the other way around. It was like we were grieving in two different languages. I could see how that might form a wedge between us, how it could create distance and hurt without anyone meaning to. Bill coped by recalling stories, listening to songs, and sharing vivid memories of Billy. That made absolutely no sense to me. To this day, he still listens to an old voicemail from Billy. He plays it often. For him, it brings a kind of peace. But for me? That would undo me completely. Just the idea of hearing Billy's voice feels like too much. For the longest time, I couldn't even look at his pictures. They were right there in the house, but I had to turn away. It was months before I could really let myself see him again. And still, even now, it takes my breath away.

We needed such different things in our grief. Somehow, we had to learn to let that be okay. While I was barely holding myself together in my own grief, we still had to figure out how to live under the same roof —both of us hurting in very different ways. We had to learn how to give each other space without pulling too far apart, and grace to grieve in whatever way each of us needed.

At that time, I had what I called the "healing room." It was this warm, cozy space tucked in the back of the house with A-framed ceilings and a big window that looked out over the lake. It felt like you could exhale there, like you'd stepped outside of regular life for a minute. The room was filled with books, old pictures, little pieces of our story, and that quiet view of the water.

Over the years, a lot of people have come through that room— for long and honest conversations or just to sit in silence. But during that season, I spent hours there by myself, trying to make sense of the deepest pain I had ever known. I was searching to find some kind of healing, or at least a place to breathe.

Right next to the healing room was a third garage. Nothing fancy, just a simple space off the side of the house. Bill's not really a handyman, but after mowing the lawn or working in the yard, he'd end up in there, puttering around. That garage became his grief place. Sometimes he'd go out there and just let it all out. Tears. Groans. Sounds I didn't even know could come from a human being. I think he believed I couldn't hear him. But I did. And honestly, I don't know what's worse—sitting in your own pain or hearing that kind of raw heartbreak come from the man you've built a life with. I caught a glimpse of his grief in those wordless, broken moments. In a very weird way, I am glad I did. I could see into his soul and it wrecked me. We were falling apart in separate rooms yet trying to survive together.

One day, Bill came back inside and the weight of the grief was too much. He dropped to the floor beside me, completely undone. Through deep, guttural cries he just kept repeating, "He was my name … He was my name …" over and over again. He could barely speak. His whole body shook with the kind of pain that comes from somewhere deeper than words. At first, I didn't understand. And then it hit me—Billy was William Elek Orris, III. Our firstborn son. He carried my husband's name. The name passed down, the name that meant something so deep, so rooted in legacy and identity.

And now it was gone. That grief—his grief—was something I couldn't touch. It didn't live in my body the way it did in his. I would never fully understand the loss he felt in that moment and for the rest of his life. And I didn't need to. I just wrapped my arms around him as tightly as I could and held him while he broke open. It was the only comfort I could offer. I tried to stay with him in the suffering I could not understand.

There were many days when we'd just sit together in the healing room, side by side, holding hands and weeping. No words. None were needed. In that silence, in all that sorrow, I knew there was no one else I would rather have beside me in the middle of such devastation. No one else I'd want to share such heartbreak with. Over the years, Bill and I have counseled a lot of young couples. I tell them every time: it's not about sex, or attraction, or how good someone looks. All of that fades eventually. I ask them, "Is this the person you want beside you if life falls apart? If you get a terrible diagnosis, or have a child with special needs, or bury someone you love—is this the one who will stay with you in it?" Those are the questions that matter. And they need to be asked long before anyone walks down the aisle.

Bill and I have found our way together over these last 10 years since our child's death. A highlight in our healing has been traveling to one of our favorite spots during the summer: the East Coast. Ocean City, Maryland, to be precise. We grew up going there, and to Wildwood, New Jersey, every year. Now we enjoy reminiscing as we stroll down the famous boardwalk with my sister-in-law and her husband. We devour the one and only east coast fries (with vinegar) and of course, the New York style slices of pizza.

Bill always heads straight for the water, and I have such joy watching him play and laugh as if he's never been there before. He loves trying to jump the waves. He is 6 '4 " and stands firm, facing every wave and staring it down as if that will prevent him from getting knocked over. Then suddenly, when I look up, he's upended with his gangly legs in the air! The waves completely crash over him and take him out! He could

7

not defeat the power and strength of those waves no matter how hard he tried.

In those moments it hit me—this is why they compare grief to waves. It rises without warning. Its rhythm is untamed as it surges and retreats with no predictable pattern to follow. Often the waves thunder in, crashing into an ordinary moment. Not every wave will undo you, but some will. And the ones that do leave you changed, forever marked by the way it rolls over your entire being, the way it completely washes you out.

Recently, I've been thinking about the big waves. You know, the ones that you can see rushing toward you in the distance. The ones that are not unpredictable but expected. You cannot stop them. They will slam right into you as if you are not even there. Seeing it coming is almost as bad as feeling its impact. These are the moments like holidays, birthdays and family vacations ... the wave is coming. So you stand there filled with dread and brace for impact.

I feel this way the first week of August every year. August 7 is my huge wave. I know it is going to roll in. I can see it forming and swelling out in the horizon days before. My heart races and anxiety fills my soul as I relive the details of that day. The day of my son's death always leaves me gasping for air as I try to keep my head above the water. Every year. Even when I can see it coming, it doesn't matter. There is no preparation. There is no trying to stand up against it. There is no finding a surfboard to make the best of it. It rolls in with a violent force to remind me that grief is relentless. And this wave of grief doesn't know how many years it's been or how hard you have tried to work your way through to find your life again. It doesn't know how many times you picked yourself back up when you had absolutely nothing left. It doesn't care.

We have obnoxious messages for people engulfed by pounding waves:

"Be brave."

"Be strong."

"You will be okay."

"You will get through this."

I don't think we would ever say that to a drowning person. And yet, this is said to grieving people all the time—the ones under water. I've tried so hard to not let grief overtake me. I've tried to dig my feet in to withstand its great force. It doesn't work. I am knocked over every single time. When that wave hits, I bear down, brace for impact, and remind myself I survived the last one. I am still here.

I am so grateful that Bill has been with me in so many of those waves. They just keep coming no matter how long it has been. The grief always remains, but it's changed. The sharp edges that once cut so deep have softened. We've learned how to carry the loss of our son—not perfectly, but with more kindness toward ourselves and each other. Our marriage looks different than it did before, and honestly, so do we. We still miss Billy every single day. That will never change. But we've found ways to keep living, to laugh again, to hold joy and sorrow all at once. We're not who we were, but we are still together, still learning, still finding our way forward.

Grief Practice: The Words of Grief

Sounds are the words of grief. They come in groans, guttural utterances, wailing, screaming, and moaning. This is why people say to us, "There are no words." At some level, everyone knows there is no way to name this kind of pain. I have written a mantra, or a prayer, if you will. We read it often together in my grief groups. It's for those moments when you have no words of your own, when nothing can describe the incredible weight you bear. Maybe these words will help hold some of that for you. It might help to repeat some of the statements on a daily basis. Affirm your grief and how you are walking through it. Put it somewhere you'll see it regularly—on the fridge, your bathroom mirror, the dashboard of your car. My hope is that these words offer you a bit of comfort, a little light, and the strength to keep going.

I am grieving.

There is nothing wrong with me and I don't need to be fixed. I am not going to apologize for my tears because they are sacred.

My tears reveal just how deeply I loved and lost.

I am giving myself permission for my pain, acknowledging that grief is a normal and natural part of life.

I do not need to deny or diminish how I feel to make others comfortable.

When insensitive comments come, I resolve to respond with kindness, knowing they do not understand.

By grace, I am committed to moving through my grief, learning every day that I do not have to remain stuck.

And through grace, I can carry my pain in ways that lead towards healing and a life that can still be good.

Chapter 2

God Doesn't Need Another Angel

Bzzt. Bzzt. Bzzt.

The texts were coming from an unfamiliar number while I was enjoying a moment I didn't want to be pulled out of: playing cards and eating pizza with my family on a perfect, hot summer evening in August. Who could need me so urgently? It was annoying, so I kept brushing it off.

Until I couldn't.

Eventually, I picked up. It was a church member.

"Pastor Lisa," he said, "a car has crashed through our church. It's in the sanctuary."

My mind couldn't keep up. What? How? Our church wasn't even close to the road. How does a car fly up an embankment, speed across a parking lot, and break through a building? It didn't seem possible. My first thought? Someone must really hate God. That level of force and direction felt … intentional.

While I dealt with logistics, my husband, Bill, headed straight to the scene. The car had slammed into the outside wall and kept going, breaking through three interior walls before coming to a stop right in the sanctuary. It was unreal, like a scene from a movie. A car—inside the church. And yet, as shocking as it was, we were overwhelmed with gratitude that no one had been inside at the time.

Both Bill and I are pastors. Many of our friends and family have said we would make a great reality show! For years, we served in different ministries, always wondering what it might be like to lead a church together. After 20 years for Bill and 10 for me, we answered a call to a congregation in the Northwest suburbs of Chicago—a community that had identified itself a "church in crisis." Something had to change or they might have to close their doors for good. So, we stepped in with great hope for this hurting church. And now a car was parked inside its sanctuary.

The crash happened on a Saturday night around 8:30. Sunday morning came at us fast, and half the building was unusable. Several leaders in our church and other local pastors offered to help, assuming we'd cancel service. But I wasn't about to let a car stop us from gathering. So we didn't.

There's no seminary course titled, "What to do when a car crashes into your sanctuary." So we worshipped outside that morning in the parking lot. We prayed for the driver. We acknowledged the chaos. And we reminded one another who God is—even when life doesn't make sense. As I was closing the service, the fire department and towing company showed up and began extracting the car from the building. It all seemed to happen in slow motion. We laughed as their timing brought some much needed levity to a very stressful situation.

That moment mattered. It marked something special in our journey as a congregation. We declared that this building isn't what makes us a church. It is not the decor, the logo, the comfortable chairs, or even the mission statement that makes us a church. That day we demonstrated a deeper connection and commitment to one another beyond the brick and mortar. We remained as one, unified and willing to stand together in the midst of chaos and uncertainty. We were—and are —the church.

I think that day they looked at Bill and I like we were going to save them. But none of us knew we would be the ones who needed saving. Five days later, on Friday, August 7, 2015, we were gathering for our youngest son's birthday. Michael was turning 21 and we were about to leave for Ravina, an outdoor music venue that sprawled across 36 acres of parkland. It was my favorite kind of day. We were dripping sweat and wearing sticky clothes. The sound of children swimming and laughing in the lake filled our ears.

When you visit Ravina, you bring all your own food and drinks. It is one of my favorite venues in Chicagoland. Lights and melodies fill the air as dusk falls. Sitting on the lawn, listening to music, sipping, nibbling—it's the perfect way to slip into a summer evening. We couldn't imagine why Michael would pick this venue. But then we learned that Harry Connick Jr. was playing there and Michael, at heart, is an old soul. We were all kind of snickering throughout the week about it, but Michael loves the classics and grew up listening to disco music with me. "Disco Inferno" was his favorite song. When he was 10 years old, he knew almost every Frank Sinatra song and could impersonate him to a T!

We were waiting for Billy to arrive at the house before we ventured out into the night. At the last minute, I was putting Michael's favorite foods in the cooler so we could celebrate with him well. I've been accused on more than one occasion by Billy and my daughter, Lauren, that he always gets special attention. What can I say? He is the baby!

As I was scurrying around, going through my mental checklist for the evening, I noticed a squad car had pulled into our driveway. I couldn't imagine why a police officer would be there. I watched as he exited his vehicle and came to knock on the door. I answered.

"Is this the Orris residence?" He asked me, nervous and fidgeting with his vest as if it were uncomfortable. "Yes." I told him, completely confused.

"Is your family in the house? May I come in?"

I began shaking as I stepped out of the way for him to enter. Bill had just come home and pulled into the driveway. He immediately came over to the door and stood by me. The rest of the family was in the living room waiting to leave. The officer stood statue-like, trying to tell us something but not quite able to find the words.

"We're waiting for our son, Billy," I said.

My heart began to race as I braced myself for what he told us next: there had been an accident.

"Where is he?" I demanded to know. "Is he okay? Is he in the hospital? Where is he?" Out of nowhere—I have no idea what took hold of me —I asked, "Is he alive?"

The man bowed his head, no. Billy had been hit and killed on his motorcycle.

The officer's voice quivered as he spoke. I could hardly understand what he was saying. I just kept screaming Billy's name as I fell to the floor. Michael darted out of the house, down the street. Bill ran into the

15

backyard and cried out in pain. There was wailing and weeping and total chaos. Our entire house was in disarray and disbelief. We could not comprehend what we were hearing. We were just about to celebrate life and now we had to go to the hospital to identify our son. Lauren, our middle child, took control over the situation—what little there was to be had of it. She drove us to the hospital, began making phone calls, and became our rock.

The entire drive to the hospital I begged God for Billy to still be alive. As I got to the room where he was lying, all I remember is leaning into the nurse who was standing by the door. I buried my head into her shoulder and sobbed bitterly. My heart could not bear what I was about to see. I remember sitting in a daze, staring at his body and glancing at the drops of dried blood on the floor that had fallen from his head. They had worked for over an hour to revive him. He was lifeless and every ounce of life left me on that day.

We spent a while in that ER room with our son. And then we had to leave. A sea of people from the church and elsewhere surrounded our home when we returned. As I got out of the car, I could barely stand up. I was weak, afraid, and in so much pain. One by one, friends held me up, put their arms around me to steady me, and got me inside the house.

Remember, I said I was a pastor. For over 20 years, my entire training and education was to serve other people in crisis. In pain. In grief. In loss. I was the one who said, "Have faith, God will work it all out." Now, I had nothing left. I didn't even want to live. I wasn't even sure I believed in God anymore. My first-born son was dead and nothing else mattered or would ever be the same. I felt like a stranger in my own life.

During the initial days following Billy's death, and during his celebration of life service, I begged every person who hugged or talked to me, "Remind me who God is. Remind me who God is." I didn't want to forget, but somehow I also didn't care anymore.

Most of the books that were thrown at me said it is a trap to believe healing is defined as the absence of pain. Likewise, faith in God doesn't guarantee good feelings, nor does it shield us from suffering. We only have to look at Jesus' life to know that is true. Experiencing the death of my son shattered my presupposed beliefs about God and how the universe works. Most of my life I have assumed God works in certain ways, ways I thought I understood and had spent years studying. My entire perspective of faith completely unraveled in a single moment, and I have spent years wrestling with whether I could believe in a God I could not understand.

In his book, Walking with God through Pain and Suffering, Tim Keller offers this: "When times are good, how do you know if you love God or just love the things he is giving you or doing for you? You don't really. In times of health and prosperity, it is easy to think you have a loving relationship to God. You pray and do your religious duties since it is comforting and seems to be paying off".[1]

What happens when God doesn't act the way we want? What happens when God doesn't support our plans or the way we think our life should go? In Elizabeth Elliot's book, No Graven Image, she writes that we treat God more like an "accomplice … someone to whom we relate as long as he is doing what we want. If he does something else, we want to 'unfriend' Him".[2] She goes on to say that most people are horrified to be asked to trust a God they cannot understand. And when we don't understand, we run the risk of becoming bitter, angry, graceless, cold, and miserable. This is especially complicated because grief and loss often lead to a confusing mix of spirituality, faith, and beliefs about God. I've encountered this dynamic so many times. It both fascinates and frightens me.

I am an on-call chaplain for two funeral homes in our community. Most of the time when I get called it is for a family that has no pastor, priest, rabbi, or other spiritual affiliation. I have often wondered, Why now? And each time, the answer becomes clear. Death shifts us into a new space where our humanity feels different and the spiritual side of life suddenly takes center stage. In those moments, people are searching for reassurance and hope because they are now faced with their own mortality. Death leaves us afraid and anxious. I've come to believe this is why "bumper sticker theology" is so appealing—it provides a sense of comfort, but often oversimplifies deep, complex beliefs.

Here's what I mean by "bumper sticker theology": people often extrapolate popular sayings that they think will make a grieving person feel better.

For example, the classic line, Oh, [the name of your loved one] is in a better place now. What does that even mean? Are they in Heaven? And why is that better than being with our family? What if your spiritual values and beliefs don't align? How is that supposed to bring comfort? People say this because it is soothing to imagine "a better place" than to acknowledge the reality that physical death is final separation and all the pain that leaves for the living. Being urged to think about our loved one in a better place does not solve our grief.

It sidesteps and silences the pain of the loss.

The tricky part is that in the Bible Heaven is described as this beautiful place with no more sorrow, sickness, pain, or tears. It is described as having streets of gold, gates of pearl, and walls made of precious stones. Dwelling there brings rest and peace. There are many books describing what Heaven is like, written by people who have nearly died and it sounds incredible! But claiming our lost loved ones are in a "better place" doesn't help the grieving person. It is a saying that can bring hurt and confusion to those who are mourning because it feels like nothing could be "better" than being together. Often, you hear people say, "This was God's will" or "God's plan." First, no one fully knows the will of God. And secondly, death is never God's will. God has always been and always will be for life … always!

One of the best comebacks to these trite spiritual sayings I ever heard was from a man in one of my grief groups whose son died of an overdose. His son struggled for years with addiction and this man is angry, bitter, and resentful. As a father, he tried everything to help his son. Countless recovery centers, tons of money for therapists, and more hospital stays than he can remember. His son left a family behind. This man is broken and searching for some kind of peace in his life.

One night another group member said, "Yeah, someone just told me that God would never give me something like the suicide of my wife if I couldn't handle it. God doesn't give us more than we can handle."

This father looked right at him and said, "So, I guess you hit the jackpot then. You are so fucking lucky that God thinks so much of you."

Of course, he said it sarcastically, but the entire group nodded in agreement. This is another example of how convoluted God and faith can become to make us feel better. In 1 Corinthians 10:13, the Bible says, "No temptation has overtaken you except what is common to humankind. And God is faithful; he will not let you be tempted beyond what you can bear." This is a verse about temptation! It has nothing to do with grief, loss, and death. And there is never an indication, Biblically speaking, that life won't give us too much to handle. It is quite the opposite.

Jesus very clearly said, "Pick up your cross." We all have crosses to bear and they are usually heavy. If we could bear everything and manage all our own problems, why would we need faith? Grieving people can barely get out of bed to face their life. We are bearing the unbearable every single day. It has always been more than I can bear. And at the same time, I know that I am only standing today because of the grace and mercy that has held me. Telling a grieving person that they are strong and can bear the pain, is like telling someone they can swim when they are drowning.

My least favorite of them all: "God needed another angel." No, God does not need another angel. God doesn't need anything. God is the Creator and Sustainer of the world. The sea, the sky, the mountains, day and night were all called into being through Divine breath. God is not a needy deity. The Source of all things gives life out of love not because of need. Acts 17:24-25 tells us, "The God who made the world and everything in it is the Sovereign of Heaven and earth and does not dwell in shrines made by human hands. Nor is this Divine One served by human hands, as though needing anything—since it is God who gives to all people life, breath, and all things."

God did not need my son. Billy's death will never be a blessing to me. There was no reason for it. There is nothing good about it. Now, it may be true that something "good" will come of his death, but in and of itself, it is not good and never will be. Grief doesn't need to be over spiritualized. We don't need to go around explaining God and how He works in the world. All these sayings only try to tame God so that we can somehow make sense of our broken hearts. It is far more healthy and real to express our anger, doubt, fear, confusion, and helplessness. Allow yourself to feel it. The problem isn't that God can't handle it. Believe me, God is more than capable. The problem is that we don't know how. We are afraid of rejection and believe that God will abandon us if we pour out our real pain because, most likely, we feel abandoned already.

My former seminary professor, Soong-Cha Rah, argues that exceptionalism in America is the problem. He calls out the American church's inability to grieve and lament:

The embedded narrative of American exceptionalism and triumphalism make it particularly difficult for the American church to practice the spiritual discipline of lament. These narratives prevent us from acknowledging the reality of suffering in the world. Exceptional people do not suffer. Exceptional people don't get sick and die.

Exceptional people do not struggle with an economic downturn. Exceptional people will inevitably triumph.[3]

Our world is suffering. People are dying. People are broken. People are in pain. Wailing and weeping seem to be the proportionate response. We are afraid to admit that we don't understand God and then proceed to spew manufactured, scripted sayings about how God works in the world. We have been programmed to use positive and peppy language, believing that is what pleases God because it's far too risky to doubt, question, or wonder if God is paying attention. This kind of spirituality is more fragile than faithful. Let's allow hurting people to grieve, lament, and wrestle with the mystery of God. Let's believe God is big enough to handle everything about our lives and is not disappointed when we struggle.

After a few months, when I tried to return to my job at the church, I remember sitting at a new members luncheon. There were about 10 people there. I was still in a daze, trying to make sense of my life, and I asked someone, "Why are you here? You realize half the church is destroyed, and our son just died."

I will never forget her response. She said, "I figured if you all can handle this kind of mess, you can handle the mess of my life too." That statement changed the trajectory of my vocation. In that moment, I knew that living out my calling would never be the same again.

When we actually stop to listen ... we encounter a God who cannot be fully understood, we discover realities that cannot be controlled, and we realize our hope is hidden not in the possession of power (or problem solving)

but in the confession of weakness.[4]

- Henri Nouwen

Grief Practice: Breath Prayer

In the early days of my grief, I felt like I could barely breathe let alone pray. Grief crushes your soul and shatters your spirit. We are made of body, mind, and spirit, and we need to let the spirit within us find its center. I was full of fear and anxiety after Billy died and felt nothing at the same time. This is when I learned about Breath Prayer, a simple way to find connection with the universe without a lot of effort or thought.

Breath prayers are short, contemplative prayers that are synchronized with the rhythm of breathing. Intentional patterns of breathing are known for positive physiological effects such as lowering the heart rate, stopping racing thoughts, and easing anxiety. They can be used to focus on specific intentions, express gratitude, or simply connect with a higher power. It is simple: match your inhaling and exhaling with a short phrase that is meaningful to you.

When we are grieving, we need simple. When my heart and mind were racing, I stopped and began to use this practice. I still do! Here are some examples:

(inhale) I surrender ... (exhale) Fill me with peace.

(inhale) I believe ... (exhale) Help me in my unbelief.

(inhale) I let go ...(exhale) Show me a new way.

Chapter 3

Your Tears are Sacred

During the first year of Billy's death, a good friend walked with me every single day. Rain or shine, warm or cold, it didn't matter. When I called, she showed up. No hesitation, no questions.

I remember those bitter winter days most vividly, when the temperature plunged below zero and the air stung our faces. We'd meet at the park, and I'd round a bend to see her waiting, wrapped in a blue parka with a fur-lined hood that almost swallowed her whole. Just the sight of that coat brought me a sense of relief. It meant she was there. I was not alone. I was safe.

One day, I texted her: "I cannot stop crying. Can you meet me at the park?"

We didn't walk that day.

Instead, she climbed into my car, and I broke. I sobbed—loud, raw, uncontrollable sounds that didn't even feel human. I wailed and groaned and screamed from somewhere deep inside me, from a place I hadn't known existed. She didn't say a word. She just sat there with me. We listened to music. She waited. I don't know how long it lasted. Time blurred. The crying stopped eventually. Somehow, I stopped.

I've never cried like that before. I didn't know I could. And I've heard so many grieving people say the same thing, with the same surprise in their voices. Like me, they had no idea that kind of emotion was even possible. It is so intense. So jagged and guttural. The kind that makes you double over and puts you face down on the ground. There are just no words to describe it. I had always prided myself on being strong, independent, composed. I wasn't the kind of woman who fell apart. I grew up in Pittsburgh—steel town, tough town.

Girls didn't play with dolls; we played with footballs. We were taught to suck it up, not to complain. Don't let them see you sweat, and for God's sake, don't cry.

My family called me "the rock." I rarely shed a tear and I wore that like a badge of honor.

But when you've spent your whole life building walls to keep pain out and something so unspeakable happens to you, they don't just crack, they collapse. You're left exposed. Vulnerable. Wide open to everything you've tried so hard to keep closed.

In grief, there is no managing. No taming. No control. The emotions come, wild and relentless, and no amount of toughness can hold them back. We are not taught how to feel. We are taught how to power up.

Ask yourself this question: What is the first thing you do when you cry in public? Apologize. In my friend Beth Miller's book, What Loss Has to Teach Us, she writes that we apologize because we have shown vulnerability, and now we feel shame. We apologize because we have exposed our deepest self and realize we have made other people uncomfortable.[1] The cultural narrative for grief contributes to the unhealthy ways in which we process our pain. Crying or showing emotion is considered weak or demonstrates deficiency.

Gender bias also contributes to holding tears back. Psychologist Judith Stillion, PhD, CT, says during childhood, boys and girls receive different messages that profoundly impact the ways they grieve. Boys, she believes, receive four fundamental messages about what it means to be a man and what constitutes proper male behavior. She refers to the first as "the stiff upper lip syndrome," in which boys are taught that men must be strong and stoical in the face of difficulty.[2] They are discouraged from expressing vulnerability and encouraged to accept pain without complaint. But men who grieve in silence—or dissociation— are more likely to participate in high-risk behaviors such as substance use after the death of a loved one.

The harsh truth is that grief is natural and necessary. It is a normal and healthy human response when someone has been ripped out of your life by death. Yet our society does not normalize grief. Instead, it pushes the message, "Just be okay. Move on." Culture has turned grief into something taboo and uncomfortable to talk about. This is evidenced in most corporations and companies' bereavement policies. Typically, when a close family member dies, an employee gets three days off. Three days to package up pain and store it somewhere else. These policies leave us with no choice but to generate a forward facing fake smile, to pretend as if our world has not been irreparably altered. Grieve in solitude. Cry when no one is looking.

When these devastating effects of grief persist, life becomes increasingly difficult to manage. It feels impossible to concentrate at work, remember to eat, or take regular showers. Judgment abounds because other people seem to think they know what you should be doing with your grief. It's called "grief shame." Grief shame sounds like:

"You should be over this by now."

"You should be moving on."

"You should be better."

"You should go out—it will be good for you."

"You should get up and get dressed."

"You should come to the party, you need to be around people."

Whenever "should" shows up, shame isn't far behind. Grieving people are already carrying so much. These critical and judgemental comments don't help—they silence and isolate us. Our pain deepens, often leading to even more hopelessness because it feels like no one understands or accepts what you are experiencing. It's hard to comprehend that something as universal as death—something that touches every single person—is met with such resistance. Even harder to understand is why we are so bad at permitting others to feel their pain.

We just don't want people to be sad. This is evidenced by the emergence of toxic positivity, and the adorning of rainbows and unicorns in every difficult situation. Our "positive vibes only" sentiment completely negates and diminishes someone's real, lived experience. The pressure to be cheerful while you are grieving makes everything even more difficult than it already is.

Emotions labeled as "negative" aren't necessarily bad for us. An entire kids' movie was made about this called Inside Out. Eleven-year-old Riley is a happy, hockey-loving Midwestern girl whose world turns upside-down when she and her parents move to San

Francisco. Riley's emotions—led by Joy—try to guide her through this difficult, life changing event. But the stress of the move brings Sadness to the forefront. When Joy and Sadness are inadvertently swept into the far reaches of Riley's mind, the only emotions left in Headquarters are Anger, Fear, and Disgust. Nobody likes Sadness. She is melancholy and well … sad. Joy always tries to cheer her up and see the bright side of life until she realizes that Sadness is an important part of Riley's life too.

Did you know crying is good for your body? Crying is a way to regulate overwhelming emotions. Cortisol—a stress hormone—is contained in your tears, so the stress literally leaves your body as you cry. Oxytocin and endorphins are also released when you cry. Physiologically, crying releases toxins. It's why people say they need a good cry! Crying cleanses your body.

April Diaz reminds us: Have you ever wondered why your tear ducts are in your eyes? Why aren't they in your armpits? If they were there, you could use some anti-tear deodorant, but no one would see them, smell them, or even know you were in pain. But they are in your eyes for that very reason. Your pain, your tears should be SEEN by someone who is looking right into your soul as you go through that pain.[3]

This is why I now boldly claim: NEVER apologize for your tears! When we grieve we allow people to see our souls, to see who we are. Crying is not a reason to feel shame. Crying is not a sign of weakness. Crying is beautiful and needed in a world full of Instagram reels that only highlight the happy parts of life. When the world shouts, "Focus on the good!" we need to be able to allow our pain—and the pain of others—to impact us, move us, and give expression to kindness and compassion.

I cry all the time now. In so many ways and places. My tears have introduced me to some of the most tender people browsing in the back of stores and waiting in checkout lines. Sometimes when I'm shopping I'll hear a song or see an item on a shelf that triggers my grief. In their kindness, strangers often offer hugs or some sort of consolation. Most people are well-intentioned. They only become judgmental or critical when they don't see us "getting better," or when they feel awkward around negative emotions. People want us to be okay. They too have been conditioned by a culture that is hurried and hoping for quick fixes and cures. Grief doesn't work that way. Healing takes a very long time. Binding wounds cannot be rushed.

Grief needs to be witnessed. Our tears aren't just sadness, they are love torn apart. When someone bears witness to that, when they stay with us, we feel seen and not alone.

But many of us grow up with very different messages. "Stop crying or I'll give you something to cry about." Sound familiar to you? That kind of language teaches us early on that expressing pain is dangerous—even shameful. We learn to hide it. Swallow it. Make sure no one sees us break.

In childhood we learn to put our pain away, to package it neatly and store it where no one else has to look at it. Eventually, even we forget it's there. But that kind of repressed grief doesn't disappear. It settles into the body. It festers. It can make us physically sick.

My counselor once gave me an image I'll never forget. He said, "Imagine your grief is a beach ball, and you're holding it underwater. You can press it down for a while—keep it submerged with all your strength—but eventually, the pressure will win. It'll come shooting up."

That's what happens when we try to avoid our pain. We don't get rid of it, we just delay the moment that it finally breaks the surface. And when it does, it rarely comes out quietly or gracefully.

A young woman in one of my grief groups lost her mother when she was just 23. The grief was crushing, but life moved quickly. She was building a career and beginning a family. There was little time to pause, let alone to fall apart. She did what so many of us do: stuffed the pain and kept going because she had to.

A decade passed. She was now a mother herself, raising two young children. And then, seemingly out of nowhere, the grief came roaring back. It didn't show up as tears—not at first. It showed up in her body. Acute stomach pain. Anxiety that wouldn't subside. Sleepless nights. A deep, persistent heaviness. She landed in the hospital. The doctors ran every test they could. Everything came back clear. No infection. No disease. Nothing they could label. On paper, she was fine. But inside, she knew otherwise.

It was only then, with nowhere left to run, that she finally admitted what she'd been carrying all those years. The loss. The sorrow. The ache of becoming a mother without her own mother there to guide her. It was in that moment that she allowed herself to finally and fully grieve. And when she did, the tears kept coming. That's the thing about grief …

it seemingly lays dormant—out of sight, out of mind. We trick ourselves into believing we are okay. The loss didn't slow us down or leave a mark.

"I went to work."

"I took care of my kids."

"I had to go on with my life."

"I don't have time to deal with anything that might affect me too much."

Until the day grief refuses to be ignored.

Healing begins when we let the tears come—unfiltered, unedited, unashamed. But to do that, we have to unlearn so much. We have to unravel the messages that taught us to stay put together. We must learn to push back against a culture that tells us to keep our suffering polite and our sorrow silenced. Grief has become privatized and highly individualized in America. Some psychologists would say we are "death averse." Lawrence Samuel writes in Psychology Today, "... in the US while we celebrate and talk about births copiously, deaths are considered an 'un-American' experience."[4]

The rise of the self—where personal emotions, thoughts, and identity are treated as the ultimate source of truth—defines much of our culture today. Yet this elevation of the individual makes it harder to face a sobering reality: our inflated sense of self, with its illusion of indestructibility, will one day come to an end. To accept that we are limited and mortal feels almost absurd against the backdrop of our self-centeredness.

"Death" and "dying" have become almost unmentionable words over the course of the last century. They're topics not to be brought up in polite conversation. Even our language of "passed away" sidesteps the obvious reality of death. A woman in my group refuses to use the term. She adamantly and passionately says her son died and is dead. She doesn't refer to his death as an "anniversary" but as a death date. She intentionally uses that language so that everyone will know and feel the pain of what happened in her family. She wants it to be jarring—because it is.

Samuel goes on to say, "Death is this country's leading source of uneasiness, discomfort and apprehension." This was not the case centuries ago. People wore black for a year after someone died. They wrote "letters of mourning" which were traditionally written on paper with black borders. The thickness of the border indicated the depth of grief. A thick black border was used soon after the death, symbolizing deep mourning. Over time, the black border would become thinner, subtly telling the reader where the writer was on their grief journey. Death portraits, also known as post-mortem photography, were photographs taken of someone who had recently died. It was not viewed as morbid. Rather, it was to preserve and remember a loved one and to honor death as a final stage of life. These were public, outward rituals and traditions that allowed people to mourn openly, to go through a process and to have their grief seen. Today this has been buried under the need for positivity and productivity. We are told to get on with our lives. Get back to the hustle and grind. Grieving takes time. It is not efficient. It does not appear productive. It seems like an inconvenience. No wonder why grief feels so un-American in this land of hustle culture.

Your tears are sacred. They deserve to be seen, but don't trust them with just anyone. Cry with those who can be present in your pain. Some do not have the needed reservoir to hold those tears with you, nor do they have the capacity to understand your journey. Your soul needs to find its way again. It takes as long as it takes.

I see this work as soul activism, a form of deep resistance to the disconnected way in which our society has conditioned us to live. Grief is subversive, undermining our society's quiet agreement that we will behave and be in control of our emotions.[5]
- Frances Wellen, The Wild Edge of Sorrow

Grief Practice: Lament

Lament is the raw, honest expression of all our emotions. It is an ancient prayer practiced by Jewish and Christian communities. It is a way to be present with everything you are feeling without condemnation and shame. While lament is often defined as a powerful expression of sorrow, anger, and grief, it usually stops there. Spiritually speaking, it is much more than that.

The book of Psalms contains 40% of laments in the Bible. Its poems cover a range of feelings from disorientation to a new orientation, distress to devotion, all rooted in the strong belief that God can handle every emotion. Rabbi Shai Held, Bible scholar and President at the Hadar Institute, says this: "The psalms show a God who can handle human rage and broken hearts. They affirm that our most savage and overwhelming emotions are also worthy material for prayer."

It is true that we often feel safer when we can express ourselves on paper, in a diary or journal. This is what the practice of lament allows us to do. We can express everything that we feel we cannot say —or should not say—out loud. The ancients instinctively knew this and practiced it repeatedly. It is a way to find your voice in the midst of complex and chaotic emotions. .

> *Healing is giving voice to the hidden parts that were shamed into silence.*[6]
> - Ellevie Parker

Try practicing the Four Elements of Lament:

- **Address**: Who are you talking to?
- **Complaint**: Describe the problem; give a brutally honest description of the events that have taken place and the emotions you're experiencing. God welcomes all feelings! He wants us to speak truth to them, so that He can draw closer to us.
- **Request**: State what you want and ask God to act or respond.
- **Expression of Trust**: State your trust and gratitude to God. At times, we can only express our desire to trust and have hope again.

Write your own. Don't hold back. Say it all!

Chapter 4

You Are Not Crazy

"Wow, you really walk a lot," my neighbor said to me.

"It's cheaper than therapy," I responded.

I was just trying to survive. Make sense of my life. I couldn't think. Couldn't concentrate. All the props I had relied on my whole life were gone. The strategies I once used to manage my emotions—those neat little drawers where everything had its place—they didn't work anymore. Grief blew up the entire dresser. Now everything was completely scattered. Socks with underwear, shirts tangled with pajamas. Nothing where it was supposed to be. Every day I had to rummage through the piles and piles of emotions to even find what I was feeling. It took longer to understand it, to sit with it, to absorb that this awful thing had really happened. These chaotic emotions, this feeling of being out of control, didn't fit into the way I operated in this world. It was like I was living in a parallel universe.

According to the Myers Briggs Personality Inventory, I am an ESTJ.

E for extraverted—I like being around people.

S for sensing— I focus on facts and details rather than abstract ideas.

T for thinking—I make decisions based on logic and objective analysis rather than emotions.

J for judging—I prefer structure, planning, and organization over spontaneity.

Before Billy died, I had no idea how compartmental I really was or how efficiently I kept my emotions stored away. Each one of those drawers inside me was carefully labeled: joy, sadness, anger, fear. I'd pull out the one I needed, feel what I was supposed to feel, then close it back up. Rarely did I open more than one at a time. I was happy when the moment called for happiness, sad when sadness was expected. They stayed organized in their separate spaces, never misplaced or messy. I thought that was normal. I thought that was control. But when death entered the room, all the drawers came flying open, spilling out everywhere. Grief, rage, anger, and confusion crashed into each other all at once.

I felt like I was losing my mind. The things that were supposed to bring joy or sadness just ... didn't. I remember staring at a stunning sunset and feeling absolutely nothing. Music, which used to stir my soul, left me numb. I went nearly a year without listening to a single song. Everything around me felt muted—dull, dark, and lifeless. In the rare moments when I did laugh or feel a glimmer of joy, guilt would creep in. How could I feel joy when my son was gone? It felt wrong, like I was betraying his memory by letting light back in. None of it made sense. On any given day, at any given moment, I was a ball of tangled mess. Grief doesn't follow rules. There are no manuals. There is no way to think your way out of it. I felt crazy but I knew I wasn't. I just didn't know how to carry so much pain.

"I'm not crazy!" is the battle cry of the bereaved. How many times do we have to say it? Grief is not a disease or a disorder. Can it affect our mental health? Absolutely. But grief in and of itself, is just that. Grief.

Depression, as one of the five stages of grief, has been more recently challenged, particularly by the Yale Bereavement Study (Maciejewski et al.).[1] Here is a list of reactions common to grievers that the study found are also symptoms of clinical depression:

- inability to concentrate
- disturbance of sleeping patterns
- the upheaval of eating patterns
- roller coaster of emotions
- lack of energy

Further, the National Comorbidity Survey of more than 8,000 subjects in the United States that met major depressive disorder (MDD) symptom criteria and whose MDD episodes were triggered by either bereavement or other loss, aged 15 to 54 years old, "… revealed that as many as 25% of grieving people diagnosed as depressed and placed on antidepressant drugs, are not clinically depressed."[2]

Mental health diagnoses can be lazy solutions thrown at grieving people with the well-intentioned—but misplaced—idea that we can get better. If grief can be labeled and categorized, then it makes more sense. If we can prescribe pills to someone, then surely they will start to move on. Everyone wants grief to be neat and tidy. Everyone likes all the socks in the sock drawer to match. But grief is always too much. It is out of control. It is intense. It goes on … and on … and on. Grief is uncomfortable —uncomfortable to bear and uncomfortable to witness. Calling someone crazy is much easier than allowing the pain to just be.

Grief is a conundrum. It's a tangled ball of intense emotions that come and go with great force. It is often far too much to try to manage. On any given day, you can be wailing one minute and laughing the next. You can vacillate between these extremes all day long. I often say, "I don't need to be fixed. I need help to navigate all the emotions that I have never experienced before at a level that feels unbearable."

What may look crazy to other people is not at all for those experiencing the deepest pain of their life. I used to think people who didn't touch their loved one's room when they died and left it just as it was for years on end were weird. I remembered people saying they often talked to their loved one while driving, walking, or running errands. That sounded weird too. Until it happened to me. Then I realized that leaving the room the way it was, holding onto that piece of clothing, and talking out loud into the wind is comforting. It helps you process the pain so that you can get out of bed in the morning.

And every person needs space to live this out, even if it makes no sense to anyone else.

Unprocessed grief is the kind of grief that experts say can affect our mental health. Fifteen percent of psychological problems are due to unprocessed grief which can lead to Prolonged Grief Disorder, a recognized mental illness (DSM-5-TR hard copy, p. 315.). This is deeply troubling to me. Why is there a time-limit on grief? Is it possible that we are stigmatizing grief as mental illness? Is our culture refusing to affirm grief as a normal response to death? Are we subtly pushing a message that tells grieving people there is something wrong with them? And does this message push people to high risk behaviors like substance use disorder and suicide?

One of the sweet women in my grief group had a son die in a car accident. She shared that she has a memorial garden to honor him on the walkway leading up to her front door. On the right-hand side, there is a huge picture of her son. She said she wants everyone who comes to her house to know that he once lived there and will always have a place in their family. A friend saw it and said to her, "Do you really think that it is healthy to have a picture of your son outside like that?"

Healthy? How does anyone know what is "healthy" when someone is grieving the loss of a child? This comment, while perhaps well-intentioned, comes from a place of ignorance. There is no "getting over" death. To some degree, it always stings, always aches. Grieving people grasp to find any way we can to ease the pain. What looks "unhealthy" or "crazy" to you, could be the very avenue we find toward peace, if that's even something we can attain at all.

I have said many times and in many of my groups that grief is the great equalizer. Your social or your financial status cannot shield you, prepare you, or carry you through grief. Your education or emotional intelligence cannot give you the answers you need. Grief comes barreling in like a storm. It violently throws you into a life you did not ask for and did not want. Death rips you out of the life you once had and forces you to figure out a new way to live. It is not a "new normal." I hate that phrase. Nothing will ever be normal again for me ... not my life, not my family, not the way I work ... nothing. There is no going back to who I was. That person is gone. My life will never be the same. I have to learn every day how to exist without my son.

If you're a grieving person, you may feel crazy, but you're not. Grief comes with disorientation and disillusionment. Your brain may feel foggy, and making seemingly easy decisions can feel utterly impossible. It's hard to know what you need or what you want. Food may feel unsatisfying and sleep is a luxury. It's as if a veil has covered everything.

In her book, The Grieving Brain, Dr. Mary-Frances O'Connor affirms why it's hard to think clearly, make decisions, or remember details and events.[3] How do you move forward in a life that no longer feels familiar? What happens when coping strategies that once worked for you suddenly fail? How do you go through each day when tears fall without warning? And how do you function at work amidst so many conflicting, chaotic emotions? Nothing seems to matter anymore. You may want to disappear without a trace. None of this makes you crazy. You are grieving. And that's okay. But remember this: There is life after death, here on earth and in Heaven. There is still joy to be found and love to be shared. Your life is different now, but it's not over.

The power of "and" changed my perspective. In the middle of all the mess, I learned that I could "be both." I could be heartbroken and hopeful. I could cry in the morning and laugh by afternoon. I could be sorrowful and still sing. It didn't have to be one or the other. I can feel all the emotions I need to, without guilt. I realized that, probably for the rest of my life, there would always be a subtle, underlying sadness even when I felt great joy. This is a difficult acknowledgement, but it also keeps Billy ever so near to me. In those moments of laughter and happiness—particularly surrounding family events like birthdays and anniversaries—my grief reminds me how my heart still yearns for him and wishes he was still with us. I don't ever want to forget. My grief keeps him close.

Grief Practice: The Practice of Welcome

A friend of mine introduced me to a spiritual practice as I was trying to navigate complex emotions. There were so many and I just didn't know what to do with them all. The utter chaos in my soul was overwhelming. I wanted to feel my grief, sadness, and pain, but I also wanted to find my way through. She said this would teach me to welcome ALL of what I was feeling without judgement or criticism.

The practice is to name, notice, and observe all of my messy emotions. To be present and acknowledge the truth of what is real. To view our emotions not as enemies but as gifts and teachers. Someone said, "Feelings are like visitors. We must allow them to come and to go." The practice of "Welcome" invites us to allow that rhythm to emerge.

Because we have lost the art of detachment, we have become almost
fully identified with our stream of consciousness and our feelings.
Don't misunderstand me; I'm not saying we should repress or deny our feelings. I'm
challenging us to name them and observe them, but not to directly fight them, identify
with them, or attach to them. Unless we learn to let go of our feelings,
we don't have our feelings; our feelings have us.[4]

\- James Finley

FOCUS AND SINK IN, THEN WELCOME

1. Do a body scan. What do you feel within yourself? An ache in your head? Twitching eyes? Pain in your neck? Heaviness in your chest? Knot in your throat? Tension in your stomach?

2. Allow thoughts and emotions to rein free for a few moments. There is so much frenetic energy in your body. Can you feel where it is? Where do your thoughts land?

3. Wherever you are drawn in your mind or body say, "Welcome, welcome." This expresses your willingness to be present with the truth of what you are feeling (and the truth sets us free). You are also welcoming the indwelling of a power greater than yourself. By saying, "Welcome," you are not trying to indulge the feeling; rather, you are consenting to the presence and action of your Higher Power, to help you with radical honesty and acceptance of where your life is right now.

Chapter 5

Suffering Is Not For Self-Improvement

As a pastor, suffering is a lot more complicated for me. I realized I'd internalized a kind of formula, one that was embedded in my theology and ministry. It went something like this: if you endure trials or testing, your faith will grow deeper, and blessings will follow. You'll be rewarded if you just stick in there long enough and don't give up. Maybe that's true in some cases. But I've come to reject the idea of "so that." You got cancer so that you can help others. You had a miscarriage so that you could become stronger. I don't think so.

The more I walked through grief, loss, and pain, the more I pushed back against the idea that Billy's death happened so that it would _____. Make me a better person? Give me a new perspective? Teach me perseverance? If that's what his death was supposed to accomplish, I wanted no part of it. I didn't want to become a better version of myself. I wanted my son back.

Yes, grief and sorrow change you—there's no question about that. But to what end? For what purpose? Is it just supposed to make me a better person? Improve my life, my goals, my outlook? If the Christian narrative of suffering is that it's all meant to make me more grateful, more "complete," and give me some sort of testimony, then honestly ... I can't buy it. I'm out.

I've found that the Christian message of suffering has been subtly reshaped to fit the cultural narrative around us. In America, the highest goal is happiness and pleasure, so it's no surprise that we've turned suffering into a tool for self-improvement. I call it "self-help suffering."

The message goes something like this: in 30 days, you can transform your grief into victory. Conquer your fears. Overcome your circumstances. Build a better, happier life. And your pain might even ease up if you just pray a little more. This language implies that we can triumph if we try harder. Suddenly, suffering becomes an infomercial … something I can consume to serve me. I wrestle with the idea that my sorrow needs to be conquered. Why must grief be something I overcome?

Dr. Paul Brand, a pioneering orthopedic surgeon in the treatment of leprosy patients, spent the first part of his medical career in India and the last part in the United States. He writes, "In the United States… I encountered a society that seeks to avoid pain at all costs. Patients lived at a greater comfort level than any I had previously treated, but they seemed far less equipped to handle suffering and far more traumatized by it."[1]

Has the church surrendered to culture by softening the reality of suffering? Have we traded the language of lament for the shallow sound bites of "think good thoughts" so that we can just be happy, comfortable, and unmoved by the pain of the world? It appears we have.

People of faith, when was the last time your church truly practiced lament? When did you last sit in stillness and reflection before the crucified Christ? We can't deny the presence of pain when the very symbol of our faith is a man nailed to a cross. Why are we so quick to shout, sing, and celebrate, yet so unwilling to sit in sorrow and admit that we are hurting? In our eagerness to pursue life, liberty, and happiness, it seems we have forgotten that the way of Jesus is death before resurrection.

If I don't rise above my grief, does that mean my faith is lacking? In some Christian circles, the answer would be yes. Our faith practice preaches grace. We are to live by it, offer it to others and ourselves. But giving ourselves grace is easier said than done. We feel the need to strive endlessly: try harder, earn the blessing, get the breakthrough. We won't admit it openly, but deep down we are trying to save ourselves by our performance—especially in front of God. And what happens when I don't "improve" on schedule? When I stay in the hurt and let the grief be what it is? When I don't "find purpose in my pain" or a "rainbow after the storm"? That is when I feel shame creep in. As if I'm doing it wrong. As if something must be so broken in me that I haven't figured out how to fix it. If I just tried harder, I could get over the death of my son. Now I am failing at grief and my faith. It is ingrained in the Christian culture—though definitely not ever said out loud—that your goodness, your merits, and your deeds should pay off. When it doesn't or when we don't get what we feel we deserve, we are angry, bitter, and resentful toward God. Maybe against everyone else, too. This was my struggle. I assumed God worked in certain ways … the ways I understood. The good people win, the bad people lose. That is what seems fair. And I am a pastor. Can you feel why this keeps getting more complicated? Pastoral work is a calling. I spent years pursuing a theological education. I devoted my life to giving to people. To helping, counseling, praying, and walking through so many of life's challenges with others. I was doing all the "right" things for God. I deserve a certain life, don't I? Well, guess what? My son was tragically killed in an accident. My good works certainly didn't pay off. Now what?

That's when it all fell apart. No matter how hard I try, there are still many days when I just cannot do it. I cannot soar like an eagle. I cannot roar like the lion. I cannot manage to put my faith over my fear or let my faith be bigger than my fear or whatever the saying of the month is. I cannot start performing in hopes that God will see all the good things I'm accomplishing and accept me. I have been wrecked by grief and suffering with zero capacity to do anything.

The only reason that I can even function today—or any day—is because of the grace of God. I should be curled up in a corner somewhere. It is nothing I did or could have done. I did not pull myself by my bootstraps or get myself through the day. I did not pray a certain way or go to church more. There is no formula or strategy to get myself right. It took becoming utterly weak, helpless, and powerless, to finally understand grace. There was nothing left inside of me to attempt managing or manipulating God into showing me favor. My sorrow and my suffering broke me. Under its crushing load, I finally learned that no matter how hard I tried at my faith, it didn't matter. It never mattered.

This is the truth about grace: it's not something I can earn. It's freely given. I am loved, accepted, seen, and known by a God of mercy and compassion, who held me in the darkness I was fighting through. I found grace in the dark. It sounds strange, doesn't it? How can there be any grace in such despair? How could I ever experience Divine help and strength when all I want to do is scream at God? Perhaps it's because that's exactly how grace comes … undeserved and unmerited. And this is the gift: in my suffering there is nothing I can do to clean myself up and be presentable. I cannot package myself so that I can be acceptable. In the anxious ball of mess that I feel on a regular basis, I experience a loving Presence that says, I know you. I see you. You are going to be okay. You don't need to get yourself together. When I allow myself to rest in that reality, I am ready to receive the gifts that come in grief.

If not for my grief, I would not have gained clarity about what matters and what doesn't. I am clearer about priorities and places I need to go. I have more compassion for others who are in pain and struggling. Grief has enlarged my soul. It has given me capacity for hard things, and the ability to help others who don't have easy answers or solutions for the unwanted things that have come into their lives. The gift of each day, with all its beauty and chaos, reminds me that I now understand what it means to live an abundant life … one full of pain, joy, sorrow, celebration, weeping, laughter, despair, and hope. Living all this, all at once, is truly a gift that only grief could give me.

Grief keeps me close to God. I am reminded that though wounded, I am not damaged. I carry grief, it does not carry me. It is part of who I am now.

In the evangelical tradition I come from, we often use language that implies a moral lesson is rooted into every hardship. The message is clear: everything that happens will somehow work out for your benefit. Theologically, that's called the Providence of God—the belief that God is behind the scenes, weaving every part of our lives into a beautiful tapestry for our good.

"God will use this season to bless you."

"Your character is being deepened."

"Once you get to the other side, you'll have such a broader perspective of life."

Do you hear it? My suffering is made out to serve a higher purpose: to make me better.

I've never liked that version of the story. It skips over the sorrow. It rushes past the pain. And it smears God's character. Jesus was called "a man of sorrows, acquainted with grief" (Isaiah 53:3). So this idea that suffering is merely a pathway to personal success stands completely at odds with the message and mission of Jesus. In fact, most of the message is about self-denial, picking up crosses, learning to be last, and losing your life to find it. Listen to what Jesus said to the disciples as he became sorrowful and troubled: "My soul is overwhelmed with sorrow to the point of death" (Matthew 26:38).

The Savior of the world—a man who healed the blind and fed the 5,000—was troubled, overwhelmed, and filled with sorrow. My counselor once said, "If you want a full picture of anxiety, depression, fear, and grief, look at Jesus in the garden." Death was near. Suffering was just ahead. He was going to die a criminal's death outside the city walls. Crucifixion was a capital punishment, the cross a symbol of shame and public embarrassment. If anyone deserved a way out, it was him. But that wasn't the mission. Like any of us wouldn't, Jesus didn't want to die in such a way. But He didn't avoid the pain—He entered it, fully experiencing grief, betrayal, abandonment, rejection, and physical agony.

Jesus' scars tell a new story. Three days after his death, He was resurrected. He appeared to His disciples, who were frightened by the sight of him. They initially thought he was a ghost. Jesus stood among them and said, "Peace be with you." Then He showed them His hands and His side (John 20:20). They recognized Him by His wounds—marks that confirmed His identity. The scars weren't concealed or avoided; they weren't a sign of weakness or shame. He literally showed them. His scars were a demonstration of shared pain and deep solidarity with his friends—and with us—in a world that is hurting.

As my colleague Ginny Aherns once said, "It was not the absence of His scars that brought recognition but their very presence." In the same way, our scars can speak truth—not just about what we've endured, but about what is being formed in and through us. We don't need to hide our wounds. What comforts me most is this: our Savior has wounds and Christ has personal experience with our human emotions. That means God is not disconnected from suffering. His wounds tell me I can trust Him—even when I don't understand. In my own grief, they are a sacred point of connection, a quiet assurance that I am not alone.

This kind of suffering was never meant as a self-improvement project. It was never about becoming a better person. Rather, Jesus intended to lead us toward becoming like Him by modeling suffering in a way that isn't about personal gain or personal glory. His mission was to lay His life down willingly, with relentless love, mercy, and truth so that others could live. Our modern-day notion of self-help suffering is completely antithetical to the message of Jesus. In his famous Sermon on the Mount, Jesus says, "… Blessed are the poor in spirit" and

"Blessed are those who mourn, for they will be comforted" (Matthew 5:4). Those who desperately recognize they are powerless to fix themselves are blessed. In these simple yet profound statements, He names the pain and poverty woven into the human experience. He's not ignoring the suffering—He's honoring it. In doing so, Jesus redefines what it means to be blessed in a world that chases success, celebrates strength, and clings to certainty. He turns the values of the world upside down, reminding us that comfort doesn't come through having it all together, but through being honest about our pain.

That is the mission I want to be a part of. That, I can say yes to. That, I can follow. If my pain, my grief, my story can somehow serve someone else on their journey, then it begins to make sense. If God can move through my wounds to bring comfort or healing to another, that feels like redemption. If my scars can be shared to lessen a burden someone is carrying, then I can know the loss of my son wasn't just about making me a more self-reliant or self-sufficient person, but someone who was able to acknowledge that suffering reveals who we really are. It exposes our limits. It knocks us off our center. It hijacks every prop we have ever used to manage our life. It strips us down to nothing. It burns down every plan, hope, and dream. And if we can look long enough, it is in the reflection of the ashes where you begin to see yourself for the first time and who you were meant to be.

Better to spend your time at funerals than at parties.
After all, everyone dies—
so the living should take this to heart.
Sorrow is better than laughter,

for sadness has a refining influence on us.

A wise person thinks a lot about death,

while a fool thinks only about having a good time.

- Ecclesiastes 7:2-4

Grief Practice: Not Forsaken

Grief reshapes who we are. It breaks us open and brings us to our knees. With our faces to the ground, we're left feeling exposed. Maybe even forgotten, abandoned, or alone. Vulnerability clings like a target on our backs. If someone had told me I was "blessed" when my son died, I might've lost it. Blessed? No. I felt anything but. I felt cursed.

When Jesus said, "Blessed are those who mourn, for they will be comforted," He wasn't talking about the kind of #blessed we see today (Matthew 5:4). In our culture, "blessed" has become a trendy caption and a decorative work on a Hobby Lobby sign. We use it to slap a superficial description on a beach vacation, a new car, or a picture-perfect moment. This is not what Jesus meant. The true meaning of blessing has been stripped down to something shallow and external. In His teachings, blessing is often tied to grief, poverty, and persecution. It's not about having a good life by the world's standards —it is God reassuring us that even in our deepest pain and brokenness, we are still loved, still valuable, and still known even when we don't feel it or believe it.

"Blessed are those who mourn" affirms that our sorrow is seen and honored. Jesus isn't dismissing pain—He's dignifying it. We are not forgotten or forsaken. Jesus Himself warned that we would face trouble

51

in this world—and He knew it firsthand. His life was marked by suffering, rejection, and loss. This kind of blessing isn't a feel-good slogan or spiritual sugarcoat. It's a profound assurance that our grief is witnessed, not wasted. It tells us that in our mourning, we are not alone, and promises that we will be comforted. We are held by God and His grace, something far greater than ourselves. We are not forsaken.

Remind yourself of these truths today, repeat them over and over again:

"I am not forsaken."

"God does not hate me."

"I am not a target for suffering and pain."

"My grief is not a punishment."

Chapter 6

Look For Beauty

Several weeks after Billy died, a good friend came for a visit. We sat
for a while and as she was leaving, she simply said, "Lisa, go look for
beauty." Intuitively I knew what she meant, but really, what did that
mean? I was never one to go out into nature or sit by a babbling brook
to hear what it was saying. I mean, who has time for that? It is a well
known fact that I am definitely not a camping kind of girl. My definition
of "outdoorsy" is sitting on my deck with a glass of wine. How was I to
look for beauty? Where was it to be found?

In the early days of my grief, nothing I saw or heard relieved any of
my pain. But in the back of my mind, I kept hearing her say, "Look for
beauty." Honestly, most of what I experienced was dull. There seemed
to be a blurry filter over everything. It was like looking through glasses
that have smudge prints all over them. I remember looking for beauty in
a sunset. It did absolutely nothing for me. I could not listen to music. I
rarely laughed. But slowly, very slowly, I started to find my way.

As fall approached, three months after Billy died, I found myself in
the backyard. Leaves were falling everywhere. I literally just stood there
and let them land on me as if they were snowflakes. My head was toward
the sky and these beautiful bright red, orange, and yellow leaves engulfed
me. Turning my attention to the ground around me, I discovered they
were shaped like hearts. At that point, this tree had been in my backyard
for five years. I had never noticed or paid attention. It was beautiful. I

found beauty and allowed it to touch my life. Before, I was too busy, too hurried, too in control. Until grief stopped everything. I was unable to keep the frenetic pace I was accustomed to. Sleep didn't even relieve the kind of exhaustion that engulfed me. There was no comparable experience, no frame of reference. I was beginning to understand why my friend's advice was important. It slowed me down - made me pause, wait, and wander. Grief forced me to be present in the moment, to pay attention to what was right in front of me.

After about six months of trying to return to my responsibilities as pastor of the church, I realized I could not function and was granted a leave of absence. During that time, I had an opportunity to go away for one week to a retreat in Tucson, Arizona at The Redemptionist Retreat facility. I had never been to the desert before. The view outside my room's window distracted me. It felt like I had landed in an alien cowboy movie. Where there were supposed to be trees and plants, there were Saguaro cacti (the large cactus with arms growing out of them), rocky sand as far as I could see, mountains, and roadrunners. (Yes, it is a real bird and not just a Looney Tunes character!) In true Lisa fashion, I went for a walk on the grounds after I got settled and found myself in the chapel. This is what I read:

The Desert will lead you to your heart where I will speak.

I will lead her out into the desert and speak tenderly to her there. I will return her vineyards to her and transform the Valley of Trouble into a gateway of hope. She will give herself to me there, as she did long ago when she was young.

- Hosea 2:14-15

I wept. It was as if the words on that wall jumped right into my heart. I couldn't believe what I was reading. As I went into the next day, I kept asking myself, What does the desert have to teach me? What is it saying? These were unusual questions—out of character, even—because I was flying through life with such speed, in a hurriedness that was exhausting and unfulfilling. I never once stopped to consider that a place or beauty or nature could actually speak to me. But now I was. And it is incredible what I discovered.

The desert is a radically different terrain and landscape from the Midwest. It felt foreign and unfamiliar. It is hard to walk with all the rocks, dust, and pitfalls that you often can't see until you are on top of it. It is full of rattlesnakes, gila monsters, scorpions, javelina, and bobcats. The spiritual director at the retreat facility would tell us to go on "sacred walks." Go out and walk with no agenda and no judgement of the process. Are you kidding me? I never just walk without a purpose! Who does that? I am a power walker who answers texts and makes calls, all while getting my steps in for the day (over 10,000, obviously).

He told us to wander. Take notice and allow our soul to go where it needs to go. Seriously, I cannot stress enough: I. Am. Not. A. Nature. Person. At. All! This was just going to be so weird and such a waste of time. In my mind, there was no way that dusty, poisonous, prickly place was going to teach me anything.

I walked around aimlessly, feeling totally ridiculous. I was beyond skeptical, and impatiently waiting for the grueling practice to be over… until I saw a humongous Saguaro. It had so many arms growing out of it. As I got nearer, I realized it was blooming. Flowers were sprouting out of the top and out of each arm. Flowers! Life in the middle of the desert! Beauty! The ugly, awful, eye sore of a cactus was blooming and it was stunning. In that moment, something deep inside my soul heard, This is you, Lisa. You think you are dead. You have always believed life equals lush —grass, meadows, green plants—but there is life in the desert. There is still life inside of you! You are pricklier now to be sure. But it doesn't mean there isn't life. The terrain of your life is completely different now and you will have to walk in a new way, but there is life to be lived.

Beauty captured me. Beauty found me. Beauty spoke to me. Beauty helped me believe. Beauty gave me life again.

I don't know what this might be for you, but I know it is imperative to look for beauty in the midst of your sorrow. We need beauty to point us toward something that transcends and illuminates the darkness and despair we are feeling when we grieve. The effect of beauty is to give us a jolt that draws us out of ourselves. Beauty reminds us that there is still life outside the hole we are in. This won't happen at first or all at once. But I promise, if you allow yourself to look for beauty, you will find it and it will fill your soul.

In my faith tradition, there is something called a "wilderness experience." Many would say that everyone on a spiritual journey goes through a kind of "wilderness," a place of nothingness, desolation, and danger. The problem is that I believed the desert and the wilderness were places to fear. In fact, I thought the desert is where you die. The desert is not a place of death. I did not go to the desert to die. I went and discovered life. A life I never knew could exist. I found my life again in that desert ... in a blooming cactus.

Though the desert works constantly to forbid it, the cactus still blooms.[1]

\- Uma Gokhale

After the tears had dried, my vision and voice became clear.
From my darkest shadow pierced the purest light.
I found myself: bruised, beautiful, and bare stripped of every comfort
but clothed in truth.
Blooming where I was once broken.[2]

\- Morgan Richard Olivier

Grief Practice: Sacred Walk

There's a story of a South American tribe that would go on days-long marches, then suddenly stop to sit down and rest for a while. After camping for a couple of days, they would walk farther. They explained they needed a time of rest so that their souls could catch up with them.

There is great value in our grieving process. When we are in pain, it's important to learn to slow ourselves and to wander about. Sometimes there is so much inner chaos that we cannot think or feel anything. Slowing down, listening, and being still helps us find our center. It helps us become present to our pain.

It's a practice I brought home with me from the desert. I often do it at my local garden nursery or one of my favorite wooded trails. When everything feels so dim and desperate, we need to allow beauty to connect us to something beyond ourselves. It's there that we're reminded that hope and healing can be found.

Everybody needs beauty as well as bread, places to play in and pray in, where Nature may heal and cheer and give strength to body and soul alike.[3]

- John Muir

Chapter 7

Into The Deep

After my desert experience, I decided it was time to go on the Lisa Live Again Tour and my closest circle of friends were eager to tag along. I wanted to do things that I hadn't done before and just go live. My young friend surprised me with front row tickets to the Brett Eldredge Glow Christmas concert at the historic Chicago Theater. What's funny about this "live again" outing is that I really don't like country music. She kept telling me, "He sounds different at Christmas!" When the curtain opened, Eldredge walked out in a purple velvet jacket with a bow tie. His swooning voice and big band sound filled the theater and to my surprise, I felt like a teenager again. It was magical!

On the Lisa Live Again Tour, we went line dancing (a first for me!), my favorite song of the night was "Turbo Twang," which my besties quickly pointed out is not even a legitimate country song. It didn't matter. I had a blast! I ate exotic food, and indulged in fancy, expensive drinks—the kind with all the colors and flowers in them. But the culmination of the tour was a trip to Israel. In my line of work as a pastor, it is strongly encouraged that if you ever get a chance to go to Israel, you go. You will walk where Jesus walked. You will see all the historical sites that you've studied for years. The Bible will come alive and change your life in ways you cannot imagine. All that always sounded like a lot of hype to me. Plus, I am an anxious traveler and had never been on an international trip. It just so happened that a couple from my church was going with another group from Boston and they asked if I wanted to join. I hemmed and hawed for weeks. I made all kinds of excuses about why I couldn't. Finally, my husband said, "You really need to go. You don't want to miss this opportunity. It's once in a lifetime!" So I did.

We went on a boat tour in the middle of the Sea of Galilee and I wept as I recalled every story and every line I had read about Jesus in this very spot. It was overwhelming. The bulk of Jesus' three years of ministry were on the shores of this sea.

Honestly, there is not much in Galilee. It is a fishing town—small, simple, and insignificant. The place where Jesus gave his famous sermon on the "mount" is just a small hillside by the lake where people gathered. The Gospel of Mark says many times that Jesus went down by the lake or taught by the lake or sat by the lake. The lake was the Sea of Galilee.

We finished our tour in the city of Magdala, on the western shore of the sea. There is a huge, gorgeous chapel that has a boat on the altar. Downstairs, there is a massive mural painting depicting the woman who touched the hem of Jesus' robe to be healed. It takes up the entire wall. All the artist chose to paint were his feet and her hand reaching for him in the crowd. It is so powerful and so moving. I stood there, gazing up at it for a long time.

As we left the chapel, I turned around and saw a Latin inscription on the top of the building: *Duc In Altum*. I turned to the tour guide and asked what it meant. He said, *Into The Deep*. I was stilled in that moment... stopped from exiting. It was as if I was held at attention in a way that I had not ever experienced. Locked into those words, I felt a movement in my spirit. The Lord gently whispered, *Lisa, you have been in the deep. It is time to go and help those who are in the deep.* I had no idea what that meant or what I was supposed to do, but I felt this new calling in the core of my being.

When I returned home to my little place by the lake in the Chicagoland area, it hit me: I live on a lake! I love my lake! So much so, my family calls me "Lisa of the Lake." You can always find me sitting on the shore. I love entertaining people there. It has been my place of peace, healing, and calm. This is what I was supposed to do: host people who are drowning in grief and pain and loss to come up for air - to find their life again.

So I did just that. Silver Lake Retreat was born in 2021. I began leading retreats for people who needed a space to breathe, to be still, and to become present to their pain so they could begin to heal.

I always thought that I was called to grow big churches and speak to large crowds. To become a Christian rockstar with a major platform that reached around the world. I think I spent most of my life chasing that in unhealthy ways steeped in performance, perfectionism, and drivenness. It got me nowhere other than really, really worn out and empty. And then I read from one of my favorite authors and spiritual companions, Henri Nouwen …

"Over the years you have allowed the voices that call you to action and great visibility to demonstrate your life. You still think, even against your own best intuitions, that you need to do things and be seen in order to follow your vocation. But you are now discerning God's voice saying ... stay home and trust that your life will be fruitful even when hidden."[1]

My grief has taught me that hiddenness is holy. My backyard, by the lake, has been a safe place for many people to process through their deepest pains; to weep, wrestle, and navigate grief. I sit with them as a companion, listening and offering guidance. Silver Lake Retreat is a step toward healing. I didn't have to go anywhere. I didn't have to search for ways to reach people out in the deep. It wasn't a platform or a social media presence that I needed to answer the call God placed on my heart. I had what I needed the whole time, right in my backyard.

Grief Practice: Retreat

Our inclination is to run from pain. I wanted to get as far away as possible, in a place where no one knew me. My counselor reminded me that no matter where you go, your grief goes with you. It is counterintuitive to turn toward our pain. Yet, leaning into it, even befriending it, can become a source of healing.

One of the best things I ever did was go away on retreats. I went to places where I didn't have to hide my pain or be okay—because I wasn't. The change of scenery and rhythm helped immensely. The beauty, nature, water, and stillness brought peace when everything inside of me felt so out of control. The space allowed me to think, pray, and shut out the noise for a few days or even a few hours.

It may seem unfeasible, or perhaps even far-fetched, that time could be set aside for retreat. It can feel like one more thing to do on an already lengthy to-do list. But I want to encourage you: find the time.

Make the reservation. Arrange your life and ask for help so that you can go. It doesn't have to be far away or long. It can be local. Take the time you think you need.

Superficiality is the curse of our age. The desperate need today is not for a greater number of intelligent people, or gifted people, but for deep people.[2]

- Richard Foster

Chapter 8

Everything Does Not Happen For A Reason

In the fall of 2022, Silver Lake Retreat was gaining momentum. Retreats were being booked and people were finding their way to my little place on the lake. We had hosted several groups including a Parenting through Grief retreat. As we approached December, I was preparing once again for our Blue Christmas program. I have led this every year since my son died. The holidays can be hard and hurtful and even more so when grieving. Where do you go when it's not the most wonderful time of the year? We provide a space where people can honor their pain and embrace hope for the future. We light candles in honor of the person or people we have loved and lost. We tell stories to encourage one another on the journey. My amazingly talented friends sing beautiful songs to remind us that we are going to be okay.

The night before the program, I was busy preparing when I got a call from Michael, my youngest son. His wife, Kierra, was in the hospital. She wasn't feeling well and had been admitted that morning, around 9 a.m. Some of her blood work had come back abnormally high on many levels. Her temperature was below normal. She had been deteriorating throughout the day. Michael kept sending updates. At 4:45 p.m., the call came.

"Mom, she is coding! Call her parents now!"

My heart dropped. I started shaking. I called my entire family to come to my house—my daughter, my brother, his partner, and my niece and nephew. One by one they arrived and we prayed. The next few hours were excruciating. Michael was on speaker phone and we listened to him speak with the doctor.

"Michael, you need to decide." The doctor finally told him. "We have been working on her for an hour and a half."

Kierra was gone. A perfectly normal 33-year-old woman went into the hospital and died in less than 24 hours. Our daughter-in-law. The mother of our twin grandsons, Micah and Malachi. My son's wife.

It was unfathomable that this was happening to our family … again. It was December 17, 2022. We had to get to Bismark. There were huge snowstorms. It was Christmas. Flights were canceled and there was no easy way to get there. We didn't get out of Chicago until the following day, on the first flight out. Landing in Fargo meant we had to drive more than three hours until we could get to our son and grandsons. The highways were horrific and probably should have been closed. I still have no idea how we made it.

How do you prepare to see your child in so much pain? He had just lost his only brother, who he was very close to. Now this? More death? More suffering? Left with two little four-year-old boys who needed their mother. Even writing this now, I feel so angry and betrayed. It felt like a cruel joke. Go ahead Lisa, help people who are grieving. Start a retreat house. Host people by the lake. Help them heal. Oh, wait a minute, here's another knockout punch. There was no way I was getting back up from this one.

I stayed in Bismarck for the next six months to help my son and grandsons find their way again. My life came to a screeching halt. The winter of 2022-2023 was record breaking, with 53" of snow in November and December alone, and dangerous wind chill temperatures on a regular basis. I literally saw tractors—the same equipment they use during harvest season—on the neighborhood streets, now "harvesting" snow. That is not normal. Schools remained open, people went to work, and the mall was bustling with early morning walkers. You may be wondering how I would know that … I admit it, I became a mall walker.

It was necessary for my mental health and my own grief, okay? One day, there was a man riding his bike up Michael's street as if it were the middle of summer. I found that so bizarre. More snow had fallen and the wind chill brought the temperature down to -20 degrees. I hate winter in general, but this particular winter held nothing for me. Everywhere I looked it was bitter, harsh, and frigid. Every day my soul felt cold and lifeless. There was no comfort anywhere. I hated all of it. I hated—and still do—that my grandsons will never know their mother. I hated that lives explode, and pieces lie all over the place. I hated how badly it hurt to pick them up. I hated that it's easier to just leave them there. I hated that every day felt like it came with far too much grief to hold. I hated that I believe God is good but could not reconcile that goodness in the face of such darkness. I hated that I wrestled every day believing and not believing at the same time. I hated that Christianity (and the Church) has perpetuated a faith that is too afraid to doubt, question, or deconstruct, leaving followers fragile and unable to handle a God who won't explain Himself.

A sign hung on the living room wall of my son's home. It is Well with My Soul. It was huge and I had to look at it every day. I could not ignore it or pretend it was not there. And nothing was well. I was not well. I felt violated and hostile. I joined the prophets in voicing my anger, shaking my fists and crying out to God from the depths of my being. I refused to be silenced by a narrative that God only wants our joyful praise and celebratory offerings. I reject that everything happens for a reason. No, it does not. Awful and horrible things happen every day and there is no reason for it. I rail against the subtle twist of the Gospel that your goodness will pay off. It doesn't. No matter how hard I try or how well I perform, painful things happen in life and it has nothing to do with whether or not I've been "good." Therefore, I will continue to lament. I will yell and scream and name every pain to God.

I will question and grope in the dark. I will weep and wail until it hurts. I will not be afraid for God to see all of me, especially in my pain. And I will do so until my soul finds God again so that maybe, just maybe, I may have a chance to be well once more.

You may think that bringing such "negative" emotions to God is wrong. But the Creator isn't afraid of the dark. We have believed that God is only interested in our perfect, shiny lives so we shrink back from bringing our full selves—every fault, every failure—because it might be offensive to One so holy. Or perhaps it lacks faith. What if the faithful response to life is pounding your chest? What if it's questioning and doubting?

The famous sufferer Job yelled, shook his fists, and gave in to every negative emotion in his being. When he finally had nothing left in him, God responded to Job and his friends, "My servant Job will pray for you, and I will accept his prayer on your behalf. I will not treat you as you deserve, for you have not spoken accurately about me, as my servant Job has" (Job 42:8). Wait, what? It seems God was pleased with Job. After all the begging, bellowing, and basically telling God he wanted to die, God honors Job. Pastor Tim Keller teaches that Job is honored because all of these negative, intense emotions were directed toward God. Job stayed in the pain.[1] Job didn't turn away. He kept relentlessly returning to God. This is so beautiful! God will not turn away faithful, honest, and raw protests. The Creator knows how we are formed and that we are dust (Psalm 113:14). We are created with all these complex emotions and we must learn how to remain in the hard ones, believing that God is right there with us and will not abandon nor punish us for feeling them.

The Church and Christianity have perpetuated the notion that we can replace every negative emotion we experience by renewing our minds (Romans 12:2). That we can "be made new in the attitude of minds" (Ephesians 4:22-23). It has been preached that we should focus on whatever is right, pure, lovely, and admirable (Philippians 4:8). If we can just do that, then all of our fear, doubt, confusion, anxiety, depression, anger, and sadness will go away. Think better, feel better. In some pulpits, "renew your mind" is treated almost like a mental self-discipline program. If you just "take every thought captive" (2 Corinthians 10:5) and replace it with truth, you'll never have anxiety, anger, or doubt again. This is demoralizing to the grieving … to the depressed and the anxious. To the fearful person who can't dig deep to find a way to get over all these feelings of torment.

Somehow the word "renew" has come to mean "remove." That was never the intended meaning. In fact, these verses, "be transformed" and "to be made new" are both present passive verbs. This means it represents the subject as being the recipient of the action. God is the one doing the transforming and renewing! We are the subject and the recipient of this action! We are NOT the ones doing it! We do not have the power to think away all of our sadness and help ourselves. In fact, Jesus stated in his famous sermon on the mount, "Blessed are the poor in spirit" (Matthew 5:3). Those who desperately recognize they are powerless to fix themselves are blessed.

Grief Practice: Solitude

At first, solitude may seem counterintuitive when it comes to grieving. Won't that make us more lonely? Not necessarily. Solitude is not about being alone or isolated. It is an intentional separation to refine and refresh your soul. Someone said, "Solitude is the soul's holiday." It is temporarily withdrawing so that you can grieve and sit with the pieces of your life. I needed to have time and space to grieve. I didn't always want to be around others.

I want to encourage you to find a spot somewhere in your home, at a park, or in the woods, and make it your own grieving place. Maybe you have candles, a picture of your loved one, or other items that might bring comfort. Let it be your time to just be.

Here are some of the benefits of practicing solitude:

• We intentionally remove the expectations of others

• We are able to hear our own heart speak

• We find rest and refreshment

• We discover that others can live without us

• We find that the world does not rest on our shoulders

• We break the cycle of busyness in our lives

Chapter 9

Find Your People

One of the most jarring and unexpected lessons I learned early in my grief journey, was that the people you believed would be there for you, often aren't the ones who can truly show up. And then, out of nowhere, others appear—people you never realized cared so deeply. It's a painful and bizarre experience. I was in the depths of my grief, and yet some of my closest people were saying and doing things that felt completely out of touch. It was insensitive and even inappropriate at times.

Someone gave me a book to read when Billy died, and one of the chapters suggested that we learn to be merciful to insensitive comforters. I threw the book against the wall. Really? I am the grieving person. My son was killed tragically. These people are being thoughtless and selfish at a time when my needs and my pain should be at the center. And now this book is trying to tell me it's my responsibility to manage the anxiety, fear, and opinions of others while I am just trying to keep my head above water? Seriously? I don't think so.

If you do not know what to say, don't say anything. There are no words. There is no making it better. Sometimes grieving people don't need suggestions, comments, or advice. Sometimes we just need you to show up.

The day after Billy died a friend came over. I had a small couch facing out to the lake in my healing room. It also had a desk and lots of books. I escaped there when I needed to think, write, reflect, or just be still. She came in, sat down beside me, and held my hand. We stared out at the lake together for hours. She never said one word. It was the most comfort I experienced in that season, and the most impactful. Job, the most well-known sufferer in the Bible, said this of his friends: "You have seen my calamity, and you are afraid" (Job 6:21). Job lost everything … houses, family members, his farm. Three friends came to visit him in the midst of his loss. Their time started out great. They sat down beside him in silence and were just present in his suffering. But then they began talking—giving him unsolicited advice and telling him to consider all the reasons these bad things happened to him. Mostly, they told him it was his fault. Maybe he didn't have enough faith or pray enough?

This is an example of what I call sympathy gone bad. It's when sympathy presents itself in the form of misguided comfort … because it is. People mean well, they really do, but they have no idea how insincere their sentiments sound. Culturally, we've been trained in the language of consoling:

"I cannot imagine how you must be feeling."

"You are strong, you will get through this."

"I am so sorry for your loss."

For the person who has just been through the tragic death of a loved one, received a devastating diagnosis, or been upended by a life altering circumstance, these well-intentioned statements sound like empty Hallmark cards. It leaves the grieving, broken person with nothing but judgement and observation about their pain. Quite simply put, this is why it feels so awful: sympathy brings disconnection, while empathy fuels connection. Brené Brown's book, Daring Greatly, helped me understand the difference.[1] When someone is showing you sympathy, it feels terrible and trite. (Trust me on this.) Why? Because often the sympathy giver has put themselves in a "better than" position. They are looking at you from a distance, both emotionally and physically, telling you how bad they feel about what happened to you.

There is no "How can I be in this with you?" It is more of an evaluation. Sympathy allows someone to remain untouched by suffering. It is far easier to stand outside of the pain and offer answers as to how this will make the grieving person "better," or give examples of how it could be worse. Neither is helpful. Job's friends could not just let him grieve. And most of the people around us can't let us grieve either.

Be aware that not everyone is able to handle your pain. Most people are afraid and anxious, often because it triggers their own fears of weakness and mortality. When you are grieving, it is critical to find your people. The ones who won't run away or give you easy answers. The ones who don't expect anything from you. The ones who send a text just to check in, not expecting a reply. The ones who just leave food on your doorstep with a note. Who go on long walks with you without uttering a word. Who hold your hand with a steady presence by your side. Who give you something to help you care for yourself. The ones who offer real help—whether it's moving, childcare, or other tasks—and show up when they say they will. Who stay consistent, even when you have nothing to give in return. Trust your instincts; you will know who you can rely on and who might be too scared to stand with you. Those who are afraid may unintentionally hurt you, and in those moments, you may need to let them go.

Susan Silk and Barry Goldman developed a simple exercise to help us know what to say, and whom to say it to, when we seek to support someone in crisis.[2] It's called Ring Theory. Basically, the person in crisis is in the middle with concentric circles around them. Each circle represents a segment of the grieving person's life: immediate family, close friends, colleagues, acquaintances. The idea is that support always goes inward toward the grieving person in the center and complaining goes out, away from them. I always tell my groups, "If people are dumping on you as the person in crisis, these are NOT your people!"

Sometimes they tell me that's great in theory, but isn't reality. A dear couple whose son died by an overdose was receiving all kinds of meals and gifts. The woman's mother-in-law said to her, "When you get time, you really need to call these people and thank them." You see, that is an expectation in a normal situation, like after a wedding shower or birthday party. The tragic death of a child by overdose is not anywhere near a typical social situation where otherwise normal etiquette and manners apply. Her mother-in-law expected her to tend to others. The Ring Theory helps us to see that support should always go toward the grieving person in the center.

Unfortunately, your people may not be in your family. This is a difficult realization, but you may have to move people who were once in the closest ring out to the margins. It is a strange phenomenon, but even during deep pain and grief, you will have the ability to discern who your safe people are. I have observed with many grieving people—and through my own grief— that we do not have the capacity to handle other people's issues, nor should we. We learn quickly, for the sake of self protection, to move those people to the outer circle. Do not feel guilty or allow people's reactions to hinder you from taking care of yourself. This is not the time to consider other people's feelings. This is not the time to engage in dialogue about their place in your life, or explain to them why their presence is hurtful and not helpful. You do not have to be mean or unkind. Just slowly and quietly detach.

How do you know who your people are? They are Miss Vickie. Miss Vickie was a stranger. She was my son's neighbor. My daughter-in-law, Kierra, had my grandsons call her Miss Vickie, a term of endearment and respect. I had heard a lot about her and her kindness toward my family. After being violently thrown into the reality of living in Bismarck after Kierra's death, Miss Vickie was now in my life too. Only she didn't use any of the familiar lingo. She didn't offer positive vibes or opinions or anything that might "fix" me. She didn't glance at me with a look that said, how terrible this circumstance must be for you. No, she was willing to be vulnerable and to risk putting herself in someone else's place. She was able to feel deeply what it might feel like to be me. My entire life came to a complete halt. I was caring for my grandsons and helping my son find his life again, away from my own home and husband. She did all of that without one word of advice. She allowed herself to feel pain, to identify with suffering, and to not be afraid of it. Her vulnerability created a beautiful, meaningful connection. Miss Vickie was neither friend nor family. There was nothing in it for her. There was no reason for her to extend such generosity and compassion. It was pure empathy.

And then there was Marilyn. I was alone in the afternoon on one of the coldest days of that winter when I heard a knock at the door. A woman who I did not know was standing on the porch. It turned out that she was the mother of someone my husband went to Wheaton College with 40 years prior! She had driven across town to give me a card and tell me how sorry she was for me and my family. I remember being so concerned that she was out in the frigid temperatures and icy roads as she was older in age. But it was the only time she could get out to do errands. Marilyn was caring for her husband, who was very ill, and there was a home health care worker tending to him. She used her only time to drive in the freezing weather to a person she didn't even know to offer comfort, support, and compassion. I wept when she left. She called me once a week until I went back home in May. These acts of empathy are what a lost soul needs the most. It is what I needed the most.

There were so many amazing, wonderful people and friends who came alongside me after Billy died. There are too many to name and I am forever grateful because they helped me heal. I mention Miss Vickie and Marilyn here because they were complete strangers ... not family, not friends. There was nothing in it for them. There was no reason for them to extend such generosity and compassion. It was pure empathy, and it brought such hope in despair.

For whatever reason, these women were willing to sit alongside me in my suffering, regardless of how uncomfortable it felt. All the while knowing there was nothing I could give them in return. Being with someone in pain isn't usually fun. It is the quiet, steady presence that says, I am not going anywhere. I am here if you need me. Miss Vickie and Marilyn stayed and stayed some more. The world needs more of them.

You got to find your people
The ones that make you feel whole
That won't leave your side when you lose control
The ones that don't let you lose your soul
You can't go in alone, everybody needs help
You gotta find your people, then you'll find yourself.
- Drew Holcomb and the Neighbors

Grief Practice: Ring Theory

Trying to figure out who your people are can be challenging and disheartening. Navigating relationships during grief can be confusing and, at times, deeply painful. You may find yourself struggling with friends or family who overstep boundaries, adding more weight to what is already a vulnerable and tender space. Grief is disorienting—it strips away your sense of stability and often leaves you feeling exposed. In this rawness, sometimes well-meaning people can misunderstand their role in your life. They may assume they're closer to you than they truly are. It's not uncommon for people to "come out of the woodwork" and insist on their connection to you or the person you've lost.

This is where Ring Theory can be incredibly helpful. Use this concept as a reference. Sit with it. Place yourself at the center, and then thoughtfully assign others to the appropriate rings based on your actual relationship with them—not how they see themselves.

Then, take a step back and reflect:

Who has been too close?
Who is offering comfort, and who is dumping their emotions onto you?
Who truly supports you, and who drains or overwhelms you?

Here's the truth: This is your time to be selfish—not in a harmful way, but in a self-protective one. Grief has put you in the center, and everyone else needs to be placed where they belong. You are allowed to move people further out, especially if their presence is causing more hurt than help.

Protect your space. This will help you find your people.

Chapter 10

The Benedictines: Presence In Pain

Since Billy's death, retreat and solitude have become regular practices
for me in my grief journey. I knew that if I was going to survive the
tragedy in Bismarck, I had to find a place to go. It so happened that my
son was in Bismarck because he is a college basketball coach. At the
time, he was at the University of Mary. One day when I was going to
campus to have lunch with him, I noticed as I trudged up a hill that to
the left there was a building that looked like a chapel. I was drawn to it
and went over to the parking lot. It was a monastery—very much like
the places I had gone many times to pray, read, reflect, and learn to be
alone with my grief. I called immediately and asked if I could do a
private retreat for a few days (a common practice at monasteries). They
had a spot for me. I planned my retreat the weekend that Kierra's
parents were coming to see the boys. I wanted to give them some alone
time, and it was an opportunity for a break for me.

Praying does not need cheerleading. This, I think, would be the
motto for the Benedictine nuns at the University of Mary. They just pray.
Every day. Every week. Every month. There is no fanfare or slick ways
to get your attention or keep it. They pray, sit with you, and allow the
words of Scripture to pour over you without explanation. The Psalms
are read antiphonally (that means they're sung) so that every day—three
times per day—you are reminded of God's word, his promises and his
law of love. These prayers are not forced or coerced on you. You are

simply welcome. It is as if the community says, This is who we are, how we pray, and how we offer ourselves to God … come and be with us. The nuns don't seem anxious or eager to over function for God. They did not rush to fix me or give me advice. Not once did anyone ask me if I was a believer. If I knew Jesus. If I wanted or needed to be saved … not once! They just showed up. Sat next to me. Guided me. Helped me. Prayed with me. Perhaps even believed for me because I could not believe for myself. I experienced them as believers who had a deep trust and dependence that God would do His work in me.

The six values of Benedictine life are: **service, hospitality, moderation, prayer, respect for persons, and community**. In all my time there, I noticed these values were not posted on the wall. They were not inscribed somewhere by an artist or boldly displayed in the lobby in large print. I was struck by that, because in my tradition, the church "mission statement" and "values" needed to be prominent so that everyone knows why we exist and what we are doing. And, they're repeated often so people will remember. I wondered if the Benedictine values were not posted because they are so deeply rooted in everyday life. They are not just nice suggestions that are easily forgotten. They are not well-crafted by wordsmiths as catchy phrases for marketing strategies. Rather, they are integrated, practiced, and demonstrated every single day. I felt received as Christ with warmth and attentiveness in a way that I had not experienced before.

That experience impacted me deeply, and caused me to pause for reflection. Too many times I have over-functioned for God, not trusting the plan and purpose for another's life. I have felt like God needed me to convince or cajole people into believing. If I could just say the right word at the right time, then I was sure someone would profess their faith in Christ. Or, if I missed an opportunity to speak about salvation, then surely it was on me that person was going to be lost forever. If I could have the right cadence, dramatic pause, or poignant illustration in my sermon, then people would be saved.

In all my years of ministry, that rarely happened. I stood in front of congregations begging people to engage in spiritual formation—prayer retreats, workshops, bible studies, and church services—almost as if my graduate degree was in cheerleading rather than theology. I often felt burned out, stressed out, and worn out. I put so much pressure on myself. I was critical of my abilities and performance. I was caught in a dysfunctional cycle of believing that it was my responsibility to make sure people found God, experienced God, and grew spiritually.

This was perpetuated by the system of the Church because often the congregation boldly voiced their dissatisfaction if they weren't getting what they wanted or needed. This continual judgement fed the beast of my own ego, exacerbating my insecurities about my ministry. What a horrible way to lead. It all feels like such a waste now. I am so angry that I allowed myself to be caught in the subtle trap which was never said out loud but certainly implied: It's all up to you. After 20 years of ministry, I wish I would have been more concerned about receiving others as Christ with warmth and attentiveness, rather than strategizing how to fit them into a mission statement. I am sure I would have done much less cheerleading.

Receiving others as Christ with warmth and attentiveness

"Let all be received as Christ."

- Rule of Benedict 53

Grief Practice: Silence

In his book, *Wild Edge of Sorrow*,[5] Francis Weller writes this in a chapter titled, Silence and Solitude: "Silence is a practice of emptying, of letting go. It is a process of hollowing ourselves out so we can open to what is emerging. Our work is to make ourselves receptive."

When we are grieving deeply, we cannot hear anything but our own pain and suffering. It bellows so loudly that it drowns out anything else that we might need to hear. Grieving especially heightens the dark, fearful voices telling us that we will never escape. In silence, we will slowly be able to discern and hear who we really are. We are wonderfully made humans with capacity for love, healing, and connection. Silence gives us room to receive what is emerging within us. The life we once knew is gone. Something new is being formed. If we can still ourselves long enough, we will hear the silence speak.

Start small. Set a timer for five minutes. Pick a word to concentrate on. When you find yourself drifting or distracted, go back to the word. Let it sink in and meditate on it in silence.

Chapter 11

Healing Takes a Long Time

I have always been a driven, focused, impatient person. I work for outcomes and look for definable growth. How else are you supposed to know if you are measuring up or not? We are conditioned to produce results because our culture attaches it to our worth and identity. We are constantly competing. Look at me! Look at what I've accomplished!

My whole life, I have been an "over." An overachiever, overthinker, overcompensator, overreactor ... I was the president of five different clubs in high school. The president of my senior class. I won the highest award in my area of study in college. The list goes on and on. You get the point. Everything I did was based on merit and how good I was at achieving. And then my son died. And then my daughter-in-law died. Suddenly, everything I had once relied on to manage my life no longer worked. Grief stripped it all away. The strategies and skills I used to stay in control were useless— because grief, pain, loss, and suffering don't respond to expertise.

Alan Fadling, in *An Unhurried Life*, calls suffering "unexpected unhurry."[1] It is so true! When death arrives, it doesn't just slow you down, it blows everything up. In our Western culture, we are not prepared for that. We're wired for progress, not pain. For moving forward, not falling apart. I had to learn—and I'm still learning—that healing takes time. A long time. You can't rush it. You can't set goals or measure progress the way you're used to. It doesn't work like that. Grief is slow, unstructured, and painfully inefficient. It doesn't fit into our culture of deadlines and doing more. It's no wonder grief often brings anxiety—we're conditioned to believe there's a "right" way to do it, or that we should be doing something to make it better. I've heard so many people say, "I thought I was doing better, but now it feels like I've taken three steps back." They say it with such defeat in their voice, as if they've somehow failed at grieving. This deep disconnect between human suffering and succeeding says a lot about how we learn to avoid pain. We want to be winning and achieving, not admitting we cannot even take the next step in front of us.

This mentality has conditioned us to strive to be the heroes of our own grief story. We live in a world that likes winners. Everybody wants to be a winner, even in grief. The hero narrative, as Dr. Frances O'Conner outlines in *The Grieving Brain*, is woven into the fabric of our culture:

> The unknowing person goes out on a journey and faces insurmountable odds with everything against them. They struggle, fight, and defeat all the obstacles which culminates in a huge celebration of victory. The person is completely transformed by all the lessons learned and comes back as the hero. There are parades, accolades, and medals awarded to idolize their bravery and courage.[2]

O'Connor writes that unfortunately, the five stages of grief have contributed to this myth. Somehow, moving through the stages has been touted as an achievement. This has had an unintended, devastating effect on the grieving and is exacerbated by others who give us deadlines. The one-year mark seems to be the biggest of all the finish lines. The expectation is that after a year, we should be moving on. Imagine how it must feel if you just can't seem to get to the next stage. Does that mean you have failed at grief? I've said it many times: I am not in a competition. I am not trying to win at grief. I am not trying to set a pace and see when I will "be better." When you are in deep pain, struggling to get out of bed, or complete simple tasks, you don't feel like a hero.

You feel broken, messed up, and unable to function in your own life. You don't want to learn any lessons or be transformed by your grief and pain. Least of all, you do not want to be told how strong you are. (Please don't ever say that to a grieving person.) And what is the real definition of being strong anyway? Grieving people say they don't have a choice.

There's a man who regularly attends one of my groups because his wife died by suicide. He has a five-year-old daughter. He often shares that his family or his boss will say, "You need to be strong for your daughter." Is he not strong because he cries every day? Is he not strong because he aches for his wife and cannot sleep? Is he not strong because he beats himself up daily, wondering why he couldn't see how much his wife was struggling? Is he not strong because he can barely explain to his daughter where her mother has gone? This is the problem with grief in our society: people want the hero. They want to see that you are conquering your pain, but they neglect the massive strength that it takes every day just to get through your life. This man is so strong. He gets up every day, gets his daughter ready for school, goes to work, makes her dinner, gets her to bed, and does it all over again the next day while grieving. He must make choices between childcare or going to his grief support group. He attends two groups regularly so that he can be a father who is present for his daughter. He wants to learn to live again and help his daughter as much as he can. When we can start defining strength this way, and not by how much someone cries, or how they measure up to time, we begin to actually see just how strong people in pain can be.

This heroic healing cultivates a craving for closure. What happens when you can't be the hero of your story? What do you do when your life has shattered beyond recognition? When you're buried under grief and loss, trying to recover but feeling like you're never going to get there? Here's the truth: the idea of "recovery" in grief doesn't work.

The word "recovery" is often used to imply that you can return to how things were, or that you can find what you've lost. But that's just not possible with grief. You can't go back to what was, and you can never get your person back. Things will never be the same again. There's no "new normal" to find. If we cannot recover from grief, then at least we can find closure, right? Everybody wants closure as much as they want to be a winner. Closure means an end, a conclusion. This is the part where we are told to pack up our pain, put it away, and be done with it. The underlying message screams: it's time to be over this now!

Pauline Boss, a social scientist suggests this: "... closure's popularity is a product of America's 'mastery-oriented culture,' we believe in fixing things and finding cures."[3] The mantra for everything that fails us is "cure and correct." There seems to be a desperation to find a cure for our grief. We want nothing more than for grief to end, but pushing for closure undermines the grieving process because it's simply not achievable.

When does grief end?

When has there been enough weeping and wailing?

How do you stop the ache in your soul?

Who can answer these questions? Closure implies completion. So, if you cannot complete your grief, where does that leave you? It makes me feel ashamed that I have something terribly wrong in my life that I just can't fix. That must mean something is terribly wrong with me. (There's not.)

A woman in my Thursday grief group lost her husband to a heart attack. They were married for 28 years and had two daughters. That day he went to work and never came home. She has spent the last four years trying to put her life back together again. She had to sell her house because the finances were a mess. The community of friends she had while she was married have deserted her now as a widow. No one calls or invites her anywhere. She finds it difficult to hold a job due to memory loss. She is constantly plagued by her mother and daughters to "buck up and get it together." This woman desperately wants to be "normal," to "recover" her life and get back to the way it was. The pressure she feels is enormous and has caused her deep shame. She feels like something is fundamentally wrong with her. But there is absolutely nothing wrong with her. Her entire life was obliterated … home, husband, friends, finances. It seems to others that it is taking a long time for her to begin healing and start living her life again. Everyone around her is anxious and wants her to pick up the pace and get back in the race.

The one-year mark seems to be the definitive time crunch. If we're not visibly improving, it's often perceived as a failure to grow or move forward. Grieving is seen as clinging to the past in an unhealthy way. One of the most common things people say is, "You're *still* grieving?"

Yes, I *am* still grieving. The person I loved is still gone. "Still" implies that grief should have an expiration date and that there's something wrong if it is prolonged. If you're "still" grieving, then you must not be improving. You must not be healing. You must not be doing it *right*.

This cultural obsession with self-help, especially when it comes to grief, isn't actually helpful at all. In fact, it often causes more harm. We learn lines like "I'm fine"or "I am doing okay," just to appease others and get them to leave us alone. It's easier to pretend you're getting better so people stop asking questions. But it's an exhausting and lonely way to live.

This push to "get better" is rooted in a culture that doesn't know how to wait. It's no wonder that those surrounding someone who is grieving often struggle. They try to apply familiar metrics like time and productivity to a process that those measurements don't apply to. I have grown to loathe words like "overcome," "conquer," "triumph," and "trending upward" as it relates to my grief. Quite frankly, as it relates to my faith, too. These words often imply steps or strategies that you implement on your own to get over your grief and pain.

There are countless books and grief experts urging us to find purpose in our pain—to uncover meaning in our loss. But what if we simply cannot? Are we supposed to wrestle some grand revelation from our suffering just to make it all make sense? The real work is learning to live in the uncertainty. To, as the poet Rilke said, " … accept the anxiety of feeling yourself in suspense and incomplete." We're not failing at grief if we don't emerge with some profound meaning. It is enough just to keep breathing in the not-knowing and the not yet. Most of us are already worn thin by the relentless, unending pounding of grief. We wake each day with heaviness on our chest, move through each moment as if wearing steel boots in deep mud, and struggle to find truly restful sleep. This added pressure to find purpose or uncover meaning can feel almost cruel.

If, along the way, something meaningful emerges—wonderful. But if it doesn't, that's okay too. It doesn't mean you're not healing. It doesn't mean you're not reclaiming pieces of your life. It doesn't mean you're not doing your absolute best to survive.

Grief is already hard enough. You don't have to prove your healing.

I think in medicine, just like in society, we see death as a failure—and we do
everything we can to avoid failure
- Shosana Ungerleider, MD, founder of End Well

Above all, trust in the slow work of God. We are, quite naturally, impatient in
everything to reach the end without delay. We should like to skip the intermediate
stages. We are impatient of being on the way to something unknown, something new,

and yet it is the law of all progress that it is made by passing through some stages of instability, and that it may take a very long time. And so I think it is with you, your ideas mature gradually. Let them shape themselves, without undue haste. Don't try to force them on, as though you could be today what time (that is to say, grace and circumstances acting on your own good will) will make you tomorrow. Only God could say what this new spirit gradually forming within you will be. Give our Lord the benefit of believing that his hand is leading you, and accept the anxiety of feeling yourself in suspense and incomplete.

-Pierre Teilhard de Chardin

Grief Practice: Untying

So many of us who grieve carry a heavy burden of guilt after the death of someone we love. The "woulda, coulda, shoulda's" replay in our minds—regrets over what we did or didn't do, say or didn't say. These feelings often start from a place of self-blame, an attempt to make sense of something that feels senseless. Sometimes, guilt feels easier to hold than the raw pain of grief and loss. Other times, it gives us the illusion of control, as if finding fault in ourselves might somehow explain why our loved one is gone. Guilt can attach itself to us like our favorite song that we listen to over and over again. At some point in our journey, we must detach and untie ourselves from it.

Find a piece of short, thick rope. Tie it in a knot. Put it in front of you and work through the following questions:

1. What is keeping me tied to my guilt?

2. Am I gaining something or getting something from holding onto it? If so, what is it?

3. Does carrying the guilt feel like I can still have power and control over my life?

4. What would it take for me to untie the rope?

Healing takes a long time. Healing is not quick and there's no finish line to reach. This practice may unfold over weeks or even months. Leave the knotted rope somewhere visible—in a drawer, on your desk, by the bathroom sink. Let it stay there as a symbol of what you're still holding.

Don't rush to untie it. Wait until you truly feel ready to release the guilt you've been carrying. When that moment comes, untie the knot. Then take the rope and let it go—toss it away as a quiet act of another step towards healing.

Chapter 12

Give Into Joy

After being away in Bismarck for six months, I returned home and collapsed on the couch, surrounded by familiar pictures that had always filled our space. Most of them were of my family—images of moments spent together, frozen in time. But now two of those faces are gone: my son and my daughter-in-law. Staring at those pictures, I felt a deep, aching emptiness. Tears came like a steady stream, unending and constant, as I tried to process the weight of it all. I was completely depleted. Numb. Disoriented. Nothing seemed right. How could I be looking at pictures of my family with two people I loved so deeply now missing from my life? All that was left were memories and photographs. It didn't seem real. It felt impossible, and yet here I was, in this heart wrenching new reality.

Once again, I was forced to move forward and find my life. But this time, it felt different—hopeless, even. There was an overwhelming sense of not caring, of not wanting to try anymore. I had already given everything I had once before and now it felt like there was nothing left.

Summer is my favorite time of year and I used it to rest and recover. The absolute best days are the ones spent floating on the lake. On those days, the water must be like glass—calm and still, without a ripple. There's nothing better than the sun warming your skin while you lie on a floatie, letting the gentle breeze carry you. Sometimes, I fall asleep only to wake up in the middle of the lake, feeling completely at ease. It's one of the best feelings in the world. That summer, I needed many of those days to heal.

As fall approached, an upsurge of anxiety began to overtake me. Until my son died, I had never struggled with anxiety. I didn't even recognize what was happening at first. There were some mornings that my heart would race and I would feel nauseous all before getting out of bed. It was an awful way to wake up. But the middle of the night was most terrifying. In the silence and darkness, my mind would spiral, rehearsing every worst-case scenario possible. My body was wrought with panic - I couldn't quiet. I quickly learned that grief is not just an emotional experience, it's an embodied response to loss. When we grieve, especially after traumatic or sudden loss, our nervous system can become dysregulated. Anxiety is a natural response to the unpredictability that grief brings. The brain tries to make sense of past events to anticipate what might go wrong next—constantly scanning for danger in an effort to stay safe. I became hypervigilant, trying to anticipate every bad thing that could possibly happen to me and nervously waiting for the other shoe to drop. After being gone for six months, everything felt uncertain. I had no plan, no direction, no clear sense of what I was supposed to do next.

The retreat house I had started was completely stalled. There were no appointments on the books, no visitors coming through the door. No meetings to attend, no retreats to plan. It felt like the groundwork I had laid seemingly vanished, leaving behind an emptiness I couldn't shake. I wasn't even sure I wanted to keep doing grief work anymore. I had fought so hard to prevent my grief from turning me cynical and bitter. I was determined to let it shape me, to help me grow in new ways and allow it to enlarge my soul. But now, I wasn't sure of anything. I had nothing left to start over.

Silver Lake Retreat sits right next door to my house. For a long time, I stared at it every day and wondered how any of it would ever make sense again. The dream that became the retreat space began on a simple, ordinary walk. That morning, for no good reason I can name, I went left out of my driveway instead of right. I remember looking down the long, steep, brick driveway of my neighbor Giuseppe. He had been so kind when we moved in—bringing fresh biscotti across the little gulley that joined our yards and telling stories about how he'd poured his heart into that house for fifteen years. He even invited us to dinner once and walking to his back patio by the lake felt like stepping into Italy— cement columns, statues, tinkling fountains, the warm smell of garlic. We ate for what felt like six hours.

We grew to know Giuseppe and his little dog, Bianca, who often got lost on our side of the yard. We slowly noticed that he wasn't well. He was forgetting things, repeating himself, and physically looked worn out. He had talked to Bill many times about how he didn't want to leave his home, which he had built with such love and care. But it wasn't safe any longer for him to be alone. He eventually had to go and live with his son.

One morning as I passed his driveway, I was deep in the kind of confusion that leads to more questions than answers, especially concerning where my life was going. Then, suddenly, a whisper: "There is your retreat house. Go ask your brother for the money." It came out of nowhere and I started to cry. I walked faster, half-disbelieving the thought. Was I really supposed to ask my brother for money?

Bob is four years younger than me, and even though he spent most of our adult lives in Seattle, we've always been close. He still teases me about the time I "abandoned" him. We had been living in Bellingham, Washington, when he came to finish college at Western Washington University. Not long after, Bill and I moved away, and he stayed. He planted deep roots there, raising his family and building a successful software company over the span of two decades. To this day, we laugh that no one really knows what Bob actually does—he likes to say he just schleps software around. But I know there's much more to him than he ever lets on.

I went to my brother with a bold ask: "Would you be willing to buy it with me?" Without hesitation, he said, "I'm in!"

From the very beginning, my brother believed in me and stood behind the mission of Silver Lake Retreat. He helped me completely renovate the sweet, cottage-style lake house. For months, we went back and forth about building a wall to create an extra sleeping area—a suite that accommodated more guests with extra privacy. The wall, the wall, the wall … it became our constant topic of conversation! Eventually, we built it, and it turned out to be a great addition that made the space far more functional. We tackled landscaping together, hauling countless loads of rocks and filling in the shoreline with wheelbarrows full of sand. Somewhere between the sweat and the sand, we had a passionate, weeks-long debate about the word "stout."

I always used it to describe someone's build—solid, strong. But he insisted it was a construction term. "That railing needs to be stout," he'd say. I kept telling him he was wrong. Naturally, it turned out we were both right.

When there are no retreats, and he isn't out of town for work, Bob lives in the house part time. I have given him the title of maintenance man, groundskeeper, and business manager, just so he remembers I am the big sister! On one of my darkest and most discouraging days, Bob came up the back steps to my house, just like he always does. That day, he sat down beside me and said gently, "Don't give up too soon." I knew what he meant. He wasn't trying to offer empty words of comfort or fix my life.

About a year and a half before my son died, his wife, Brenda, died suddenly and tragically. She hadn't been feeling well, and when my brother returned home that afternoon, she was gone. In an instant, he became a single father to two children. I went out there to help in the first few weeks, but I had no idea how to ease the depth of his sorrow. Watching him in so much pain was unbearable. It was first of the many tragedies to hit our family.

When he told me not to give up too soon I knew he spoke from a place of deep understanding. He knew better than anyone that grief can feel like it will destroy you. He had been through his own heartbreak, and now, he saw that this was another crushing blow for me. In that moment, for that one second, his words and presence were a glimmer. It provided something that I did not have inside of me. His tenacity and determination to not let me give up was a hint of hope that I needed to keep moving forward. When we are deep in grief and overwhelmed by pain, our nervous system is on overload. It's essential not to overlook the small moments—the flickers of light that break through the darkness, the quiet whispers of encouragement, the tiny sparks that somehow keep us going when we feel completely done. These brief but powerful bursts of comfort help regulate our system. They remind us we are safe and not completely lost. My brother was the glimmer I needed that day. He believed for me when I couldn't believe for myself. And he still does.

If you suddenly and unexpectedly feel joy, don't hesitate. Give in to it. There are plenty of lives and whole towns destroyed or about to be. We are not wise, and not very often kind. And much can never be redeemed. Still life has some possibility left. Perhaps this is its way of fighting back, that sometimes something happened better than all the riches or power in the world. It could be anything, but very likely you notice it in the instant when love begins. Anyway, that's often the case. Anyway, whatever it is, don't be afraid of its plenty. Joy is not made to be a crumb.

- Mary Oliver

Grief Practice: Glimmers

Glimmers are micro-moments of grief relief.

Unlike triggers, which stir up pain or distress, *glimmers* are tiny sparks of peace, safety, or joy that offer comfort in the midst of grief.

Rooted in Polyvagal Theory—a concept introduced by Deb Dana—glimmers are those small but powerful moments that help regulate your nervous system.[1] They gently guide you back to a sense of connection, calm, and grounded well-being. Glimmers are small moments of positivity that help soothe us in the midst of difficulty. They can be as simple as spotting a rainbow or hearing your favorite song. These brief experiences may seem small, but they can make a big difference.

Glimmers activate what's known as the *ventral vagal state*, a part of our nervous system associated with safety and connection. In this state, the body responds with lower heart rate, reduced blood pressure, and decreased cortisol levels, helping us feel more regulated and at ease.

Here's how to practice:

See:

• Start by becoming aware of tiny moments that feel good, comforting, or peaceful.

• Don't judge these moments for being small, just name them.

Savor:

• Pause for 10-20 seconds and really take it in.

• Breathe deeply and let the feeling settle into your body.

Spark:

• Surround yourself with small things that spark calmness: a cozy blanket, favorite music, a pet, nature, photos of loved ones.

• Build small rituals into your day to make room for glimmers

Examples of Glimmers

• Sunlight through the trees
• A warm drink in your hands
• A hug or gentle touch
• A moment of eye contact

• A favorite song or smell
• A deep breath that feels grounding
• Laughter (even if it's brief)

Chapter 13

Grief Guide

As I was trying to regroup and rediscover my life, a major milestone
loomed ahead—my 60th birthday. I decided to get away for a few days,
hoping for a little space to breathe and reflect. While I was away, I heard
someone casually mention that they only had 14 summers left. At first, I
didn't understand. But then he explained: the average life expectancy is
74.6 years.

That hit me like a lightning bolt.

I was about to turn 60. If I only had 14 summers left, how was I
going to spend them? There would be no more waiting for "someday,"
no more putting things off until next year. This was the final stretch of
the journey, the last act, the third-third. I had to make it count. In that
moment, I made a decision. If I was going to take a swing, I was going
to swing hard. No holding back. No playing it safe. It was time to take
risks, step forward, and pour everything I had into what mattered most.
I was drained—physically, emotionally, spiritually—with no clear
direction. Yet this pull to keep showing up for those who grieve and to
fiercely advocate for those who feel marginalized by their pain wouldn't
let me go. I was sure I had nothing left to give. I questioned whether I
could keep going. This work is demanding. It costs something deep and
personal every time I lead, speak, or sit with the grieving.

So I started asking myself the harder questions: What am I really here
to do? What is my true calling? How do I want to live the next 14

summers of my life? I had circled countless possibilities over the years, but slowly, a deeper truth emerged: I'm not a therapist. I'm not a coach. I'm not some kind of grief guru. I am a guide.

I guide people through grief. Like a seasoned white-water raft guide who's navigated the rapids again and again, I've traveled the river of loss. Now, I'm here to journey alongside others—each with their own unique story—helping them find their way through the turbulent waters. Making sure that even in the deepest waves, they feel safe, supported, and never alone.

This realization made me feel like I had finally touched something I had been grasping at for years, but couldn't ever reach. I didn't fully understand what being a "guide" meant, but something inside me recognized it. There had been so many false starts, so many ups and downs. Tragedy upon tragedy stalled my life. Still, something felt like it was rising up. A huge pivot was ahead. I wasn't certain, but I could sense it: everything I had done up to this point in my life was converging here. The purchase of the retreat house, 20 years of pastoral ministry, being present with grieving people at the lake, creating a sacred and safe space … it was all becoming clear.

Once again my brother came up the back steps. Only this time, he had sketched out an entire business plan on pieces of a cardboard box held together with blue painter's tape. (I literally have saved it! It is priceless!) We had little resources and operated on a strategic shoestring budget thanks to Bob. He repeatedly reminded me that we were woefully underfunded (which he still does!), but with the help of talented family members and others around me who believed deeply in the mission, Grief Guide was launched.

While the retreat house has served an amazing purpose in helping people heal, (and it is still available for special events or one-on-one processing), it became apparent that retreats and retreating are difficult concepts to communicate to people.

What do you do on a retreat?

Why do I need a retreat from my grief?

How will I make time to retreat?

The idea of "retreat" seemed to be creating a barrier. It became clear that we needed a broader stroke if we were going to actually help grieving people. Grief Guide brought into sharp focus that our mission was to guide grieving people whether they be individuals, companies, or communities. We now offer different ways people can connect with us.

Support groups are offered three nights per week every week. There is no fee or registration. We intentionally wanted to make it easy and accessible. No one who is grieving is thinking clearly, and the last thing we wanted was for people to have to worry about money. There is no curriculum so there is no commitment to attend a certain number of groups for a determined amount of weeks. We do not promote formulas or strategies to "get over grief." We believe in a lived experience. Each of us are on our own journey and we share what is helping us find our way through with others.

We also offer grief awareness training. As I've said in several different ways throughout this book, our culture is horrible at grief. Grief awareness is not just compassion, it is a skill that can be learned.

Whether you're a caregiver, leader, educator, coworker, or friend, this training was designed to prepare you for those uncomfortable moments when you just don't know what to say or do. Grief Guide wants everyone to do better for the people they love.

Finally, grief retreats are still part of the mission. This is offered as a deeper, intensive focus on the grief journey. A retreat is a set apart, sacred space to allow your pain and loss to find rest. We believe that stillness, solitude, and nature's beauty play an integral part in the healing process. Typically, there are three to four teaching sessions led by seasoned grief guides. We also incorporate grief practices, allowing people to explore varied expressions of their grief whether through art, writing, creating, or smashing stuff!

In January of 2024, I was asked to attend and present at our county's People in Need forum. Over 800 people attend this event every year to discover and learn about available mental health resources and other services. I was slated to speak in the last session of the day at noon. No one had ever heard of Grief Guide or of me. For that reason, and the topic, I was sure no one would show up. To my surprise, the room was packed! I was completely overwhelmed and energized at the same time. I think what I knew deep down all along was proving itself … people do want to talk about grief, loss, and pain. They just need permission and a place to do it. At the end of my presentation, I asked if I could say a blessing over them, just because our world is filled with so much cursing. There was a resounding, "Yes!" I read the Griever's Prayer that I wrote (see Chapter 1). People were visibly moved. It was then that I knew Grief Guide was going to be special.

That event propelled Grief Guide into wider visibility in our community. Requests to present to hospitals, organizations, and at various venues filled my inbox. I was finally getting to say all the things that I've wanted to say for years, and it was being so well received! Grief is a topic no one wants to touch. It's too much, too intense, too uncomfortable. But what I discovered is that in my community, and within society at large, grief is overlooked and underrepresented. For the past year, I've been pounding the pavement, putting myself out there and advocating for grieving people. I've been waving the flag and ringing the bell about how our collective avoidance of grief and pain is harming not only individuals, but the very fabric of our society. My mission is to make grief normal. By doing so, we can help one another in more compassionate and gentle ways. We must do better, and Grief Guide exists to ensure that we do.

Deep in my soul I also knew that what was unfolding wasn't just a grieving mother's attempt to "find meaning," or create a passion project in her son's memory. This wasn't about making something good out of something devastating. Every time I gave a presentation, I could feel something powerful happening in the room. My raw, lived experience resonated with my audiences and struck deep chords. I could feel my words breaking open the cultural narrative around grief and loss, challenging the tidy, time-bound version of healing we've all been taught to expect. Every time I say, "Never apologize for your tears!" there is usually a spontaneous eruption of applause from the audience, and some even allow themselves to shed a tear or two. It's a kind of release —a quiet permission to feel pain. So many people walk through life bottled up, shackled by silent suffering, trapped in an invisible prison where grief and heartache have no place to breathe.

In a society obsessed with positivity and the pursuit of happiness, there's little room for sorrow. But when we give voice to pain, when we name it and let it be seen, something sacred happens. People exhale. They soften. They remember they're not alone. They finally feel free and not forced to hide. I have watched it over and over again. As I speak, I don't just see faces, I see hearts holding stories. I believe that for some, simply sitting and listening stirs a grief they've never fully faced before. It may be the first time they've allowed themselves to feel it and even recognize it for what it is. Grief has a way of lying dormant until something—someone—gives it permission to surface. And sometimes, all it takes is hearing someone else's truth for our own to begin breaking through. Grief doesn't always hit us at the funeral. We are often too numb. Often in shock and reeling from the devastation we are experiencing, desperately wanting it all not to be true. It is in the moments where I'm sharing my own pain that I know deep in my soul I am doing what I am supposed to.

The best part of my work is sitting in support group circles surrounded by grieving people. We currently lead about 13 groups each month, serving approximately 75 people. Each participant carries a unique loss and is at a different point on their grief journey. I intentionally keep our groups between eight and 10 people, as I've found larger groups can make it harder for individuals to open up and share. While some may feel they should only be with others who have experienced the same type of loss, our experience shows otherwise.

Time and again, participants tell us that hearing different perspectives and coping strategies has been invaluable to their own healing process.

I always say the members of these groups are some of the most beautiful people I never wanted to meet. They have endured trauma, tragedy, suffering, and loss. Our conversations immediately go deep. There is no time for managing an image or pretending. Death has devastated them. Their emotions are raw, expressed through swearing and weeping. Some are surprised at how open they are to strangers. But I always tell them, "Deep speaks to deep, pain speaks to pain. You don't have to sit in that circle and explain your pain. While our relationships with grief may look different, we all know what it's like to be scarred by it."

There's an unspoken trust and a deep sense of being believed and seen in these circles. Clear affirmation and validation of grief is exchanged. Nothing is wrong, too much, or off-limits.

In one of my groups, we share the personal rituals we have with our loved one's remains. Where is the urn placed? How do they touch, speak, connect with their person? To someone outside that circle, that might look unhealthy or strange. But that's not true. This practice allows for us to actively move through grief. I don't believe in formulas, strategies, or prepackaged curriculums for grief. The healing process begins when we show up to interact with grief in real time. What mends us further is the support we receive by others walking the same road.

One of my favorite quotes from Francisian priest, Richard Rorh, says it best: "People who are too nice and never suffer or reveal their own negative emotions usually do not know very much about themselves—and so the rest of us do not take them too seriously."[1]

I take every one of those beautiful people in my groups seriously. They are full of wisdom and profound insights. I listen to them speak with every ounce of my being. They teach me and help me so much!

I'm frequently asked, "Will I always feel this way? Will it always hurt this much? Will the pain ever stop?" My answer is this: grief softens over time, but it will always be with you, which is why we need to learn to integrate it into our lives. This is not about balancing our life between grief and no grief. This is not about recovery. We can never recover the people we lost or the life we had. This is about rebuilding and adjusting to a completely different life. Things will never feel the same, and trying to force life back to how it was only deepens the suffering.

Many grieving people have shared with me how significantly they've changed after loss, and how they're learning to lean into those changes. Some who were once extroverts now find comfort in solitude. Some who lived as workaholics have slowed down to notice the small, sacred details of life. Others who were once critical now show up with compassion and tenderness. Some who were obsessed with pleasing others have discovered that most opinions don't matter as much as they thought. And those once consumed by money or material success have come to see what truly matters most.

None of us would have ever chosen these changes outright. We certainly would not have wished for the pain that brought them on. But if we're willing to turn toward our pain, we might discover that there are gifts in grief. Since my son died, I am not the same person and I don't want to be. Grief has changed me—formed me into someone who feels more honest, more grounded, and less guarded. The worst has already happened. I can't be shattered in the same way again. I'm no longer easily offended, hurt, or shaken by things that once mattered so much. They just don't carry the same weight anymore. I now hold life very loosely. There's a strange freedom in that.

One of the best books I've read on my journey is *A Grace Disguised* by Jerry Sister. He lost his mother, wife, and a child in a singular accident, leaving him a single father to his three remaining children. I held on to this statement for dear life: " … the life you had envisioned will never be but it doesn't mean it still can't be good."[2] When Billy died, I had to come to terms with the fact that all of the hopes and dreams I had for my life and family would never come to be. But I held on to the belief that it could still be good. Here is some of the good:

- Bill and I just celebrated 39 years of marriage.
- My youngest son, Michael, has remarried a tender, sweet young woman. She has embraced our family and given us another grandson, Theo. Michael would say she is his angel that came to earth. He continues to pursue his career as a college basketball coach.
- My daughter, Lauren, has been a pillar of strength, friendship, and faithfulness to Bill and I. She often says she never wanted to be the oldest as she quite liked being the only daughter in the middle of two sons. However, she has willingly and amazingly stepped into that role with so much grace and love. She works as an Events Manager for a nonprofit organization in the

western suburbs of Chicago and she helps me a lot with Grief Guide. And she lives nearby, which is a gift.

This is not what I had envisioned for my life. Yet every day I choose to look around and say it is good.

I imagine you may be wondering where I stand these days—with my faith, with the church, and with God. The truth is, I've pushed hard against easy Sunday school answers and the overly spiritualized clichés that often get tossed around when it comes to grief. None of that held up after my son died. Honestly, it didn't help and actually pushed me away. It all sounded so hollow: do this, say that, believe this, everything will be fine. But grief doesn't follow that formula. And neither does God. I've been face-down on the floor more times than I can count. I've tried to outrun the pain. I've yelled, cussed, and pleaded—sometimes all in the same breath—just trying to make sense of it all. Nothing about this has come quick or easy. And God didn't show up the way I had once studied, prayed about, or even preached.

Here's what I've come to believe: God does not willingly inflict pain, heartbreak, or sorrow. This world is bruised and broken. Terrible things happen and far too often. The universe is too vast for me to claim any real understanding, let alone try to explain it—biblically, theologically, or spiritually. Blaming God is easy. But I've learned to stop demanding explanations and start understanding who I am in this world.

Job has helped me with this. After 35 chapters of Job pouring out his guts, pleading for answers as to why God would allow for all of his suffering, he finally gets a response. God says, "Where were you when I laid the foundation of the earth" (Job 38:4)? Then God walks Job through a series of questions about the creation of the world, the boundaries of the sea, the rising of the sun, the storehouses of snow and hail, the paths of stars and constellations. On and on it goes. The point is this: God is Creator, Sustainer, and Provider. No words are big enough to contain the depth, the magnitude, or the mystery of the Divine. God is beyond full comprehension, yet intimately near. This was Job's response...

> *I know that you can do anything, and no one can stop you.*
> *You asked, 'Who is this that questions my wisdom with such ignorance?' It is*
> *I—and I was talking about things I knew nothing about, things far too wonderful*
> *for me.*
>
> - Job 42:2-3

When I read that, I too knew I had been talking about the things of God—things that I really knew nothing about. You see, religion likes certainty. Religion likes rules and boundaries. Who's in and who's out. Religion is constructed in a way that can be measured. As a trained pastor, the church has set me up to make sure that I have the answers and that I hold the measuring stick. But I don't. Job thought he understood how God works in the world, until he encountered the depths of suffering.

Jesus is so difficult to understand. In the book of Luke, an "expert" of the Law approaches Jesus and asks, "Who is my neighbor"? The question demands a definition. Religious people need to know how to fulfill the requirements of the Law. Are they living up to the standard? But Jesus' answer completely flips this question on its head.

He tells the story of the Good Samaritan. In it, a man is beaten, robbed, and left for dead. Two religious leaders pass him by, but a Samaritan—a person considered an outsider and enemy by the Jews—stops to help. The Samaritan tends to the man's wounds, brings him to safety, and pays for his care. Jesus' answer shocks the expert. Instead of defining who qualifies as our neighbor, He calls us to be a neighbor that embodies mercy, regardless of who stands before us.

Most of us hear the story of the Good Samaritan and immediately want to identify with the hero. We want to be the one who stops, helps, and shows compassion. We certainly don't want to be the priest or the Levite— the ones with status and titles who walked on by. But I believe we must start somewhere else. Before we can be the Good Samaritan, we need to see ourselves as the one lying on the road. Beaten. Powerless. Vulnerable. Desperate. Until we do, we'll keep living with the illusion that we know better than God and that we can provide everything we need for our life. Loss thrusts us onto that road—often without warning and against our will. Yet there's beauty and good news for us: Jesus walked down that road. He entered into my suffering. In all my pain, doubt, anger, and emptiness, I had nothing to offer him. I could do nothing to earn his love. But because of Great Love, I was not rejected or abandoned. He tends to my wounds. He holds me safe in his arms.

He provides care for my spirit.

I've come to accept that life will hold both beauty and devastation. But even in the wreckage, I believe in a Creator who meets us there—

with mercy, grace, and compassion—especially in the depths of our despair. We are not forsaken.

I didn't set out to start a nonprofit. I set out to survive and to find my way back to myself. But somewhere along the way—through the ache, the unrelenting questions, the quiet moments of grace, and the people who showed up when I needed them most—I realized that my story wasn't just mine. Grief Guide was born not from answers, but from many sleepless nights fraught with fear and anxiety about how I was going to keep going. Elisabeth Elliot, whose husband was killed along with four other missionaries in Ecuador, says that her life was completely controlled by fear after her husband died. Every time she started to step out to help others, fear stopped her. Then a friend told her something that set her free: "Why don't you do it afraid?"

Every person on this journey wonders the same things:

Will I survive?

How will I make it?

How will I keep going?

How will I wake up and face another day?

Will it always hurt this much?

I've asked those questions too, and on some days, I still do. I wish there were a manual or a step-by-step plan with all the answers. But grief doesn't work that way. It requires you to live through the most unbearable, unimaginable thing that has ever happened to you. I didn't find my way out of the darkness—I found my way through it. At the beginning of every support group, I light a candle. I say, "No matter how dark it may seem, no matter how deep the hole feels, no matter how much despair you feel, the candle reminds us that the light will always shine in the darkness and the darkness will not overcome it."

Grief Guide is here to hold the light until others can see it for themselves again. And maybe, just maybe, the next weary traveler will be able to find their way back to a life that can still be good.

Scan the QR code to explore more resources, videos, and interviews at https://app.mygriefguide.org/book

Works Cited

Chapter 2

1. Keller, Timothy. Walking with God through Pain and Suffering. Dutton, 2013.
2. Elliot, Elisabeth. No Graven Image. Fleming H. Revell, 1966.
3. Rah, Soong-Chan. Prophetic Lament: A Call for Justice in Troubled Times. IVP Books, 2015.
4. Nouwen, Henri J. M. Life of the Beloved: Spiritual Living in a Secular World. Crossroad, 1992.

Chapter 3

1. Miller, Beth Taulman. What Loss Can Teach Us: A Sacred Pathway to Growth and Healing. Upper Room Books, 2021.
2. Stillion, J. M. (1985). Death and the sexes: An examination of differential longevity, attitudes, behaviors, and coping skills. New York, NY: Hemisphere Publishing Corporation.
3. Diaz, April L. "What Our Tears Mean." AprilDiaz.com, 9 July 2013, https://www.aprildiaz.com/articles/what-our-tears-mean.
4. Samuel, Lawrence R. "Death 2.0." Psychology Today, 29 Jan. 2014, www.psychologytoday.com/us/blog/psychology yesterday/201401/death-20.
5. Weller, Francis. The Wild Edge of Sorrow: Rituals of Renewal and the Sacred Work of Grief. North Atlantic Books, 2015.
6. Parker, Ellevie. Quote.

Chapter 4

1. Maciejewski, Paul K., et al. "An Empirical Examination of the Stage Theory of Grief." JAMA, vol. 297, no. 7, 21 Feb. 2007,

pp. 716–723. American Medical Association, doi:10.1001/jama.297.7.716.

2. Wakefield, Jerome C., et al. "Extending the Bereavement Exclusion for Major Depression to Other Losses: Evidence from the National Comorbidity Survey." Archives of General Psychiatry, vol. 64, no. 4, Apr. 2007, pp. 433–440. American Medical Association, doi:10.1001/archpsyc.64.4.433.

3. O'Connor, Mary-Frances. The Grieving Brain: The Surprising Science of How We Learn from Love and Loss. HarperOne, 2022. 4.4. Finley, James. "Don't Make Much of It." Center for Action and Contemplation, 26 Apr. 2023, https://cac.org/daily meditations/dont-make-much-of-it-2023-04-26/.

Chapter 5

1. Brand, Paul, and Philip Yancey. Pain: The Gift Nobody Wants. Zondervan, 1993.

Chapter 6

1. Gokhale, Uma. "The desert works constantly to forbid it, and still the cactus blooms." Art print by Uma Gokhale. Quote.

2. Olivier, Morgan Richard. Blooming Bare. Concise Publishing, 2021.

3. Muir, John. Our National Parks. Houghton Mifflin, 1901.

Chapter 7

1. Nouwen, Henri J. M. The Inner Voice of Love: A Journey Through Anguish to Freedom. Doubleday, 1996.

2. Foster, Richard J. Celebration of Discipline: The Path to Spiritual Growth. Revised edition, HarperOne, 1998.

Chapter 9

1. Brown, Brené. Daring Greatly: How the Courage to Be Vulnerable Transforms the Way We Live, Love, Parent, and Lead. Gotham Books, 2012.

2. Silk, Susan M., and Barry Goldman. "Ring Theory of Support: A New Tool for Surviving Grief and Other Traumas." Grief Digest, vol. 17, no. 1, 2011, pp. 1–5.

Chapter 11

1. Fadling, Alan. An Unhurried Life: Following Jesus; Rhythms of Work and Rest. InterVarsity Press, 2013.
2. O'Connor, Mary-Frances. The Grieving Brain: The Surprising Science of How We Learn from Love and Loss. HarperOne, 2022.
3. Boss, Pauline. "Ambiguous Loss and the 2020 Pandemic." Mind of State, mindofstate.com/ambiguous-loss-and-the-2020-pandemic transcript/, 2020.

Chapter 12

1. Dana, Deb. The Polyvagal Theory in Therapy: Engaging the Rhythm of Regulation. W. W. Norton & Company, 2018.

Chapter 13

1. Rohr, Richard. "A Surprising Command." Center for Action and Contemplation: Daily Meditations, 1 Mar. 2024, https://cac.org/daily-meditations/a-surprising-command
2. Sister, Gerald L. A Grace Disguised: How the Soul Grows through Loss. Expanded ed., Zondervan, 2004.

About the Author

Lisa Orris has experienced deep grief. For over 20 years, she has walked with people through all kinds of pain, giving them permission to feel. She is the founder of Grief Guide, a nonprofit organization dedicated to guiding people, organizations, companies, and communities through grief. Lisa's work has gained her recognition in her local community where she was recently named one of McHenry County, IL Women of Distinction in 2023. Lisa is an ordained minister in the Evangelical Covenant Church.

Lisa holds a Master of Divinity from North Park Theological Seminary. She spent her undergraduate years at Gannon University earning a degree in Criminology. Lisa has presented on the county level at the People in Need Forum, Community Connection Summit, and most recently, at the Psychiatric Nurses Association (IL) at Roosevelt University.

She is married to Bill, the chaplain at Northern Illinois Recovery Center, and has three children: Billy with the LORD, Lauren, and Michael. Her big joys in life are twin grandsons, Micah and Malachi, and baby Theo. When she is not writing, speaking, or guiding people, Lisa loves to take long walks, linger by the lake, and enjoys good Italian food!

www.ingramcontent.com/pod-product-compliance
Lightning Source LLC
Chambersburg PA
CBHW060636130626
46555CB00002B/832